A gift for:

From:

SITTING IN GOD'S SUNSHINE . . .
RESTING IN HIS LOVE

ALICIA BRITT CHOLE

Published by the J. Countryman division of the Thomas Nelson Book Group, Nashville, Tennessee 37214.

Published in association with the literary agency of Alive Communications, Inc., 1465 Kelly Johnson Blvd., Suite 320, Colorado Springs, CO 80920.

Project manager: Terri Gibbs

Cover designed by The Design Works Group, Sisters, Oregon.

Photo of Alicia by randybacon.com

ISBN: 1-4041-0175-6

www.thomasnelson.com
www.jcountryman.com

Printed and bound in China

DEDICATION

While writing *Sitting in God's Sunshine*, I felt led to picture my precious baby girl as a grown woman and write to her. So these words reflect the truths I long for my daughter to embrace.

My prayer is that I'll be there to walk with her in her adult years. But if not, may these principles of resting in God's truth guide my dear Keona to follow Jesus faithfully until we resume our walk together on the other side of this life.

Baby Keona, *Sitting in God's Sunshine* is dedicated to you!

Love,
Mommy

CONTENTS

RESTING IN GOD'S LOVE

RESTING IN GOD'S FORGIVENESS

RESTING IN GOD'S WORD

FOREWORD

One of my greatest problems is my heart—a heart that gets carried away with loving people, with wanting to bless them, and consequently finding it hard to say "No"—or feeling guilty when I do! My other major problem is I think I can do more than I can.

Both of these came into play when I shared the platform with Alicia, heard her speak, and realized how much she loved the Lord and His Word. When Alicia asked if I would write the forward to her book—I said "yes." How could I resist?!? I was taken by this dear woman—of course I would.

When the manuscript arrived in the midst of an overwhelming schedule I thought, "What have I done?"

Out of duty—not delight—I picked up the manuscript. I was relieved when I saw that it was a compliation of short insights on different topics. I formed a strategy for getting it read—but it was unneeded.

The minute I started to read my heart and soul were taken captive. As Alicia began to minister to me with her incredible insights into my Father's precious Word, I knew it was of God that I said yes. I read in awe. I thought *I wish I could write like this—so succinctly, so powerfully, so practically!*

It was immediately apparent that Alicia had spent hours at our Father's feet, that she had worked through the text—studying it and internalizing it—and that I, like you, dear reader, would be the blessed recipient of what this precious woman had so bountifully harvested from God's bread of life, the Word of God.

This is a book I'll turn to again and again . . . it could become a classic.

–Kay Arthur

PREFACE

What is *rest*? A dreamy dessert? Longed for, but only considered after a hearty main course, if we have space, if we have time, and if we can splurge a bit.

A rare reward? A much deserved bonus bestowed sparingly upon a few who have obviously gone above and beyond the call of duty through decades of faithful service.

A lost luxury? The blessing of a simpler day before technology ushered us into 24/7 productivity.

I believe that true rest is none of the above. Neither optional nor outdated, not a relic of the past or available only in retirement, rest is an essential part of God's daily rhythm for our lives.

Sitting in God's Sunshine is a journey toward rediscovering the riches of resting in God and His Word. This book echoes an invitation Jesus gave to us thousands of years ago:

> *Because so many people were coming and going
> that they did not even have a chance to eat, Jesus
> said to them, "Come with me by yourselves to a
> quiet place and get some rest." Mark 6:31*

Away from the noise,
away from the crowds,
away from the rush and the loud voice of need.

Resting in God is like sitting along the ocean shore as the sun rises. So my friend, pull up a chair and crunch your toes into the warm, welcoming sand. Listen to the gentle roar of His Word. Bask in the healing strength of His Truth.

The change we all long for is not found in going faster. Lasting transformation is the fruit of resting in God's truth.

–Alicia Britt Chole

God calls us to come
away with Him.

RESTING IN
GOD'S PRESENCE

~

A SOOTHING SUMMONS

Jesus said, "Come to me, all you who are weary and burdened, and I will give you rest. Take my yoke upon you and learn from me, for I am gentle and humble in heart, and you will find rest for your souls. For my yoke is easy and my burden is light."

—MATTHEW 11:28–30

"Come," Jesus calls to us, "come and get some rest." His invitation stirs a longing deep within. We desperately desire rest for our cluttered minds and tired hearts. Let us examine more closely this soothing summons of Jesus.

Come to me, all you who are weary and burdened, and I will give you rest. Jesus calls to Himself those who are *weary* and *burdened*. The Greek word translated *weary* (*kopiaō*) describes those who are tired from hard labor or emotional fatigue. *Burdened* refers to *carrying a heavy load*. Jesus uses this word once more in Luke 11:46 where He rebukes the religious leaders because they, *"load people down with burdens they can hardly carry."*

16

So if you have been working hard and are tired, if you are discouraged and feel weighed down under many responsibilities, this invitation is specifically for you!

One remedy alone exists that can refresh a weary spirit. Rich cream can relieve dry hands and a hot bath can comfort aching bones, but only the God who created us can breathe new life into the depths of our being. There are no substitutes for His Presence.

Jesus makes this clear: *"Come to Me,"* He says. *"I will give you rest."* This would be false advertising if Jesus were only human, but since He is God we can take this as a firm and faithful promise. God Himself is the singular source of rest for the soul.

Take my yoke upon you and learn from me. After hearing Jesus offer us rest, somehow *take my yoke* is not the next phrase we expect to hear! Yokes are wooden frames placed on the shoulders of oxen to help them pull a heavy load together. Used figuratively in New Testament times, yokes could refer to judgment, submission, service, or duty.

Jesus tells us that yoke-free living is not the cure for our weariness—being yoked to Him is. As we submit to Jesus, serve Him, and learn from Him, we will discover spiritual rest. How?

I am gentle and humble in heart, and you will find rest

for your souls. For my yoke is easy and my burden is light. Serving is not wearisome when the One we serve is loving. In the world, a servant's job it to make life better for his master. But in Jesus, we have a Master who works to make life better for us, His servants.

Jesus' leadership serves us well. Because He is gentle and utterly selfless, submitting to Him increases, not depletes, our emotional and spiritual reserves. The yoke He offers is *easy* (*chrēstos*); it is good and kind. Jesus' leadership is benevolent. Unlike an earthly employer, He never breaks our backs for His benefit or profit. Anything He asks us to carry is light because He chooses to carry most of the burden Himself.

In this passage, Jesus teaches us that the source of true rest is submission to His gentle leadership. "But," we may ask, "if serving Jesus leads us into rest, why do so many of us who follow Him still feel deep weariness in our souls?" Perhaps in part because we submit to many other things besides Jesus. Such as . . . worry, other people's expectations, bitterness, legalism, ambition, and fear. These masters are merciless. They take and give nothing in return.

But Jesus gives more than we could possibly return. He is a gentle master. As we unyoke ourselves from masters that only take and yoke ourselves to the One who always gives, Jesus' leadership will refresh our weary souls.

- ☼ *Only God's Presence can refresh our spirits.*
- ☼ *The surprising source of that refreshing is submission to the gentle leadership of Jesus.*
- ☼ *Yoked to Jesus, the weary in mind and body can find true rest.*

GOD'S PRESENCE IS ENOUGH

"My Presence will go with you, and I will give you rest."

—EXODUS 33:14

"God, with all due respect, You either have the wrong person or Your timing is way off," we whisper, shaking our heads in disbelief. But His will keeps pressing on our hearts, calling us to dream with Him again, calling us to do the impossible.

"Maybe in the past or in the future . . . perhaps if I had more experience or fewer birthdays . . . possibly if I possessed greater gifts or lighter responsibilities or . . ." our excuses are endless.

But God does not expect us to evaluate the unknown future and calmly conclude that it is manageable. He is not asking us to place our abilities on one side of the scale and His calling on the other and declare that they balance. They do not balance, and they never will!

So if not in a sober, reasonable, accurate estimation

of our aptitude, what does God expect us to hold on to in order to risk following Him into the unknown?

Moses had the same question. He was an eighty-year old shepherd whose dreams had died decades earlier. Then one day God showed up as a fire in a bush and called Moses to lead a nation of slaves out of bondage.

> *But Moses said to God, "Who am I, that I should go to Pharaoh and bring the Israelites out of Egypt?" And God said, "I will be with you."* (Exod. 3:11–12)

There it is! What does God expect us to hold on to in order to risk following Him into the unknown? *His presence!* His calling always includes His presence.

In the dialogue that follows, Moses basically says, "Thank you, but Your presence is simply not enough." Now Moses does not say this directly, but he clearly implies it. How? The same way we do; he continues to make excuses:

> *"Suppose I go to the Israelites and say to them, 'The God of your fathers has sent me to you.' And they ask me, 'What is his name?' Then what shall I tell them?"* (Exod. 3:13)

Interpretation: I do not know You enough to do this!

> *"What if they do not believe me or listen to me and say, 'The LORD did not appear to you'?"* (Exod. 4:1)

Interpretation: No one is going to believe that You spoke to me!

> *"I have never been eloquent, neither in the past nor since you have spoken to your servant. I am slow of speech and tongue."* (Exod. 4:10)

Interpretation: I do not have the gifts to match this calling!

> *"O Lord, please send someone else to do it."* (Exod. 4:13)

Interpretation: I am too afraid!

With infinite patience, God perseveres in calling Moses, and Moses eventually yields. In the months and years that followed, Moses witnessed the fulfillment of God's promise to deliver His people from bondage. He discovered that God had the power to keep His Word.

Over time, something began to grow in Moses' heart—something called trust.

Later, we are able to listen in on another, very different, conversation between Moses and God:

> *Moses said to the* LORD . . . *"If you are pleased with me, teach me your ways so I may know you and continue to find favor with you. Remember that this nation is your people."*
>
> *The* LORD *replied, "My Presence will go with you, and I will give you rest."*
>
> *Then Moses said to him, "If your Presence does not go with us, do not send us up from here."*
> (Exod. 33:13–15)

In Exodus chapter three, Moses was certain that God's presence was not enough. Thirty chapters later, Moses was certain that God's presence was all he truly needed.

Thankfully for Moses, and for us, God does not expect us to have chapter 33 confidence in chapter 3. When His calling presses on our wavering hearts, He answers our questions with, "I will be with you." As we risk following Him into the unknown, He offers His presence. It *is* enough.

☼ *God does not expect us to evaluate the unknown future and calmly conclude it is manageable.*

☼ *God does expect us to take hold of the promise that His Presence accompanies His calling.*

☼ *God's Presence is with us through each faltering step, and that is enough.*

THREE WAYS TO BRING GOD JOY

The LORD takes pleasure in His people.

—PSALM 149:4, NKJV

What an inspiring truth: God takes pleasure in us! The word translated *takes pleasure* appears elsewhere in Scripture as *accepts*, *delights*, and *enjoys*.

Though imperfect and in-process, we give God joy! How can that be? Scripture identifies several ways we can bring gladness to God's heart. Let us consider three:

Fear the LORD and hope in His mercy.

> *He does not delight in the strength of the horse; He takes no pleasure in the legs of a man. The LORD takes pleasure in those who fear Him, in those who hope in His mercy.* (Ps. 147:10–11, NKJV)

The strength of the horse and *the legs of a man* were the measure of any army in the Psalmist's day. But our strength, speed, and strategies are not a source of joy to

SITTING IN GOD'S SUNSHINE

God. He does not take pleasure in mighty armies that inspire fear but in human hearts that fear Him.

The fear of the Lord is not currently a popular topic. Though we might prefer to define *fear* as "respectful friendship" the word still means "to be afraid." After all, He is God and we are not. He is pure and we have sinned. The fire of His holiness would surely consume us were it not for His mercy demonstrated by Jesus on the cross. Is God lovingly near? Yes. He is near AND He is not us. Truly, His awesomeness makes His nearness all the more precious.

God also takes pleasure in those who *hope in His mercy*. Hope speaks of *waiting for*. We only wait for something if it is not here yet. Patiently waiting for God to demonstrate His unfailing love brings God joy. Faith that can breathe in the gap between "what we hope for" and "what we now see" pleases Him.

Be just in all your business dealings.

> *The Lord abhors dishonest scales, but accurate weights are his delight.* (Prov. 11:1)

Misleading would be a fair substitute for *dishonest*. Sincere mistakes are not the subject of this passage. God is clearly addressing intentional deception. In this Proverb, Solomon is referring to unethical practices in the marketplace. Many merchants used two different sets of weighted stones: "Lighter stones were placed on the scales when selling (so that a lesser quantity was sold for the stated price), and heavier ones were used when buying (so that more was obtained for the same price)."[1]

Most of us do not spend our days sitting on a mat with scales and stones measuring out questionable quantities of rice. However, God's eyes still search for honesty in our business practices.

In our offices, do we let people weigh/credit us for more (or others for less) than we know is accurate? Do we use different stones when weighing the time we spend working for an employer than the time others spend working for us?

God hates dishonesty disguised as profit. He takes joy in accurate, fair business dealings.

Receive God's gift of forgiveness.

> *"I say to you that likewise there will be more joy in heaven over one sinner who repents than over ninety-nine just persons who need no repentance."* (Luke 15:7, NKJV)

Here Jesus gives us a glimpse into what heaven treasures: the repentance of sinners. Which makes sense since Jesus did not die on the cross so that we could be beautiful or talented or entrepreneurial or wealthy. He died so we could be forgiven.

So for Heaven's sake, get forgiven! The heavenly host does not rejoice over self-righteous souls falsely comfortable in their seemingly spotless lives but over sinners who repent. When we come before God seeking His forgiveness and cleansing, we acknowledge and honor the sacrifice of His Son and that most certainly brings Him joy.

All of us long to experience the joy of God's presence. But Scripture assures us that—by fearing God, waiting for Him, being fair in the marketplace, and receiving His forgiveness—our presence can bring Him joy as well.

☼ *We can live in a way that brings pleasure to God.*

☼ *He takes delight in those who honor His holy presence.*

☼ *Repentant souls, balanced scales, and hope-filled hearts bring God joy.*

---

[1] Walvoord, J. F. Zuck, R. B., & Dallas Theological Seminary. 1983–c1985. *The Bible knowledge commentary : An exposition of the scriptures.* Victor Books: Wheaton, IL

THE JOURNEY BACK
FROM COLLAPSE

The LORD said, "Go out and stand on the mountain in the presence of the LORD, for the LORD is about to pass by."
—1 KINGS 19:11

lijah was absolutely exhausted. He had faced and defeated 450 false prophets. He had climbed a mountain to earnestly intercede for drought-ending rain. He had run for twenty-five miles faster than the King's chariot. And now, in what should have been a moment of victory, wicked Jezebel sent word that she was planning to kill him.

That was it! He was done! The combination of post-ministry exhaustion and fear of man was just too much. Elijah ran for his life, *"and prayed that he might die. 'I have had enough, LORD,' he said. 'Take my life; I am no better than my ancestors.'"* (1 Kings 19:4)

Though few of us have faced several hundred prophets of Baal, we do understand extreme weariness. The stresses of work and finances, the strains of relationships and conflicts, and the realities of spiritual opposition leave us feeling fatigued. Add a crisis to that normal load and we can collapse altogether.

How did Elijah journey from collapse to having the strength to obey God again? Typically to answer that question we turn to Elijah's encounter with God on Mount Horeb. But even before his incredible mountain experience, Elijah was regaining strength in small and seemingly insignificant ways in the desert. How?

1. **Elijah prayed.** After running from Jezebel, an isolated Elijah plopped down under a scruffy tree in the desert and prayed. Yes, it was a pretty miserable prayer, but he was still talking to God and every little bit helps!

2. **Elijah slept.** No instant cures exist for fatigue. Our bodies cannot be plugged into an outlet and revived in an hour. There are no substitutes for time and rest.

3. **Elijah was touched by an angel**. When we are exhausted, God sends His messengers to us in many forms: the hug of a child, a call from a friend, the touch of a loved one. God's arms are long enough to reach us, even in the desert.

4. **Elijah ate.** Some of us wish we would lose our appetite! But for those of us who actually do, we must remember to eat. In his state of weariness, Elijah enjoyed angelic cuisine.

5. **Elijah encountered God on the mountain.** After a very long walk, Elijah arrived at Mount Horeb. God instructed him to, *"go out and stand on the mountain in the presence of the LORD, for the LORD is about to pass by."* (1 Kings 19:10–11)

There Elijah saw a shattering wind, an earthquake, and a fire, *"but the LORD was not in"* them. During these three powerful events Elijah heard NOTHING—which could have been a bit frustrating. So perhaps we should not be surprised when we hear nothing also. And perhaps we should be encouraged that in the midst of silence—even when it is the last thing we want to hear—something in the waiting still works to strengthen our souls.

God was in the gentle whisper. There God and Elijah exchanged the identical dialogue they had in the cave:

> Then a voice said to him: *"What are you doing here, Elijah?"* He replied, *"I have been very zealous for the LORD God Almighty. The Israelites have rejected your covenant, broken down your altars, and put your prophets to death with the sword. I am the only one left, and now they are trying to kill me too."* (1 Kings 19:13–14)

Creativity runs low when we are exhausted. So Elijah

repeated his previous response: "I have done my best but nothing seems to make a difference. I am all alone and some people would be happier if I were gone."

Elijah's words have not changed much from his prayer under the tree in the desert but his weariness has obviously subsided because when God gives Elijah directions, the prophet has sufficient strength to obey.

Certainly the concentration of God's presence on the mountain strengthened Elijah, but God's presence in the desert carried him there. In minute yet meaningful ways, God's presence was refreshing Elijah all along as he slept and ate, walked and prayed, was touched by angels and waited for God to speak.

As we journey from collapse back to a point where we have strength to obey, let us be careful not to underestimate the desert. The mountain is amazing, but the desert is equally full of God's presence to refresh our lives.

☼ *God can bring us back from collapse.*

☼ *The journey back to strength includes prayer, much rest, good food, long walks, and the touch of a few "angels."*

☼ *In the desert as well as on the mountain we find restoration in God's Presence.*

GOD SEES THE HURTING

She gave this name to the L<small>ORD</small> who spoke to her: "You are the God who sees me," for she said, "I have now seen the One who sees me."

—GENESIS 16:13

Whom does God see?

In Genesis 16, God seeks out a fear-filled woman through the first-recorded appearance of the Angel of the Lord. This same Angel would later visit Abraham, Isaac, Moses, and Gideon. In each encounter, these individuals knew they had been in the presence of God Himself.

But before the Angel of the Lord appeared to Patriarchs, Prophets, and Mighty Warriors, he first visited a frightened slave girl named Hagar. She emerged from that experience certain that the God of Creation personally had His eyes upon her: *"You are the God who sees me."* By studying Hagar's life, we gain insight into the "me" that God sees.

God sees those who are far from home. Egyptian Hagar was purchased as a slave by Abraham's household.

Her name—which could mean *flight* or *stranger*—is Semitic (not Egyptian). She probably received it from her owners, not her parents. When sold into slavery, Hagar left everything behind: her name, family, culture, and dreams.

God saw Hagar, and God sees us: His eyes are upon us when we are in unknown territory.

God sees those who have had choices stolen from them. Perhaps Hagar was sold to pay her family's debts or perhaps her parents were also slaves and had no say in the matter. Whatever the circumstances we can be confident that unmarried Hagar did not volunteer for slavery. She had no choice. And freedom would not be the only choice taken from her.

Hagar became Abraham's wife's maidservant. A stunning woman, Sarah had everything but a child. Though God had promised the couple an heir, Sarah grew impatient. Looking to the pagan culture for direction, she sent Hagar to sleep with Abraham in the hope that she could have children through her slave acting as a surrogate. Abraham did not object, so Sarah gave Hagar as a concubine to her eighty-five-year-old husband.

God saw Hagar, and God sees us: His eyes are upon us when—through abuse or betrayal, rejection or oppression—others take our treasure to spend on themselves.

God sees those who harbor pride and resentment. Though some choices were stolen from Hagar, one choice would always be hers: the choice to pollute her heart or to keep it pure. She chose the former path. Scripture explains that Hagar conceived, but, *"when she knew she was pregnant, she began to despise her mistress."* (Gen. 16:4) Once pregnant, Hagar no longer saw herself as Sarah's slave but as Abraham's more prominent wife and she acted arrogantly toward her barren owner.

God saw Hagar, and God sees us: His eyes are upon us when—regardless of our reasons—we caress sin in our souls.

God sees those who have been hurt by His people. At this juncture in the story, it would be wonderful if Abraham and Sarah had responded with such godliness that Hagar, inspired by their example, released her arrogance and anger. But that is not how God's people responded. The rivalry between Hagar and Sarah intensified to the point where Sarah, with the full permission of her husband, *"mistreated"* Hagar. In the Hebrew, this word speaks of *punishing* and *inflicting with pain.* These wounds from God's people were two-fold: Sarah verbally and probably physically abused Hagar, and Abraham— the father of her child—refused to protect her.

God saw Hagar, and God sees us: His eyes are upon us when His people wound instead of heal.

God sees those in impossible situations. Pregnant, hurting, and horribly alone, Hagar fled into a hostile wasteland. Going forward would kill her body. Going back would kill her heart. There, exhausted from sorrow, she collapsed in utter hopelessness on the sand. There, in a spiritual and physical desert, the God who sees spoke to her.

God saw Hagar, and God sees us: His eyes are upon us when our hope runs empty.

God saw Hagar then. God sees us now. He sees us when we are far from home. He sees when choices are stolen from us. He sees when we sin, and He sees when others sin against us. Our God sees all who are in impossible situations, and His Presence still fills hopeless hearts with a singular, transforming truth: *You O God are the One who sees me!*

☼ *God sees all of us; the hidden, the hurting, and the marginalized.*

☼ *God speaks to Patriarchs and slave girls alike.*

☼ *When hope runs empty, we can take heart: God knows our name and His eyes are upon us.*

FORGOTTEN, BUT NOT LOST

"I will not forget you!"
—ISAIAH 49:15

"Where could they be?" we mumble, rummaging through that catch-all drawer, "Matches . . . cough drops . . . a screw from who knows where . . . an old button . . . but where are they?!" We made them for such a time as this, when we misplaced (okay, lost) our primary set of keys. So we made a spare set of keys just in case. And we put them—now where did we put them? Not in that drawer, not in the tool chest, not in those magnetic boxes that always fall off, where on earth did they go?

Have you ever wondered if God feels like an extra set of keys to us? Not our first preference, but where we start searching when all is lost. We look here, there, trying to remember where we last left Him. But, as with the spare keys, He has not moved, we have. As with the spare keys, He did not forget, we did.

Looking through the Old Testament, we come across

several pages that are stained by God's tears: *"Does a maiden forget her jewelry, a bride her wedding ornaments? Yet my people have forgotten me, days without number."* (Jer. 2:32)

How can we forget God? All too easily.

We forget Him when we look around at God's blessings and act as though we attained them on our own.

> *When I fed them, they were satisfied; when they were satisfied, they became proud; then they forgot me.* (Hos. 13:6)

We forget God when we find hope for the future in our wisdom or our wealth instead of in His love and mercy.

> *You have forgotten me and trusted in false gods.* (Jer. 13:25)

We forget God when we lose the memory of His past faithfulness in our lives.

> *They forgot the God who saved them, who had done great things in Egypt, miracles in the land of Ham and awesome deeds by the Red Sea.* (Ps. 106:21–22)

We forget God when we take the beauty He gave us and spend it pursuing the world.

*"She decked herself with rings and jewelry, and
went after her lovers, but me she forgot," declares
the* LORD. (Hos. 2:13)

We forget God when we return to things and places
that once turned our hearts away from Him.

*My people have forgotten me; they burn incense
to worthless idols, which made them stumble in
their ways.* (Jer. 18:15)

We forget God when we think we have to provide for
ourselves through unethical practices.

*You take usury and excessive interest and make
unjust gain . . . and you have forgotten me,
declares the Sovereign* LORD. (Ezek. 22:12)

We forget God when we wake up rushed, find a few
minutes to read the world's news, but cannot spare the
time to read His news.

Be careful that you do not forget the LORD *your
God, failing to observe his commands, his laws
and his decrees.* (Deut. 8:11)

We forget God when we fail to remember where we would be without His mercy.

> *Be careful that you do not forget the* LORD, *who brought you out of Egypt, out of the land of slavery.* (Deut. 6:12)

The good news is that even though we may have forgotten God, He NEVER forgets us: *"Can a mother forget the baby at her breast and have no compassion on the child she has borne? Though she may forget, I will not forget you! See, I have engraved you on the palms of my hands."* (Isa. 49:15–16)

That extra set of keys in the drawer may be lost forever, but God's presence—though forgotten—is never utterly lost in this life. God has not moved. He has not forgotten. While we have breath, there is still time to remember Him again. And in remembering, we soon realize that not He but we were lost and now are truly found.

☼ *Our busy, wandering hearts often fail to remember God's goodness.*

☼ *God is not immune to pain; He aches when His people forget Him.*

☼ *Even when forgotten, our gracious God never forgets us.*

STRENGTH TO SERVE

*Now in the morning, having risen a long while before day-
light, He went out and departed to a solitary place; and
there He prayed.*

—MARK 1:35, NKJV

In Mark 1:21, Jesus entered Capernaum with his newly
called disciples and stepped into the swift current of
service. On the Sabbath, he was teaching in the synagogue
(exhausting enough) when a demonized man interrupted
his message by shouting, *"What have we to do with You,
Jesus of Nazareth? Have you come to destroy us? I know who
you are—the Holy One sent from God!"* (Mark 1:24, NKJV)

Some disruptions can be gracefully ignored, but this
disruption was about as ignorable as a lion in your living
room. One obviously had to address the situation so Jesus
silenced the spirit, commanded it to leave, and *"the evil
spirit screamed and threw the man into a convulsion, but then
he left him."* (Mark 1:25, NLT)

So much for discrete spiritual confrontations! Everyone in the synagogue witnessed this rather spectacular

encounter and soon everyone in Capernaum and the surrounding cities heard about the amazing Teacher who had authority over evil.

Leaving the stunned crowds, Jesus entered the home of Simon and Andrew and found another person in need. Simon's mother-in-law had a serious fever. Jesus took her by the hand and she was healed! (Mark 1:29–30) Many healings are gradual but this was instantaneous. Simon's mother-in-law did not simply sit up to cautiously sip from a bowl of chicken noodle soup. Completely restored, she got up to wait upon her guests!

So, in summary, on that day the crowds were taught, a demonized man was delivered, and a sick woman was healed. Now it was time to eat and relax and sleep. As the sun set, the Sabbath ended . . . and Jesus and his friends heard a knock on the door. Scripture tells us that on the other side, the entire town was waiting. After ministering far into the night to the sick and oppressed, Jesus finally laid down to sleep.

However, long before the sun rose, Jesus got up and quietly slipped away. Yesterday was spent with the masses, but the new morning begins with time alone. Yesterday was filled with teaching, but the new morning begins with listening. Yesterday was flooded with activity, but the new morning is marked by waiting: *"Now in the morning, having risen a long while before daylight, He went out and departed to a solitary place; and there He prayed."* (Mark 1:35, NKJV)

A wise friend once offered this counsel: "Balance travel with stillness, speaking with silence, and the crowds with solitude." Jesus modeled this balancing rhythm in His earthly ministry. We regularly find Him withdrawing from the many to rest with the One He called Father.

Here, in the protected place of private prayer, Jesus found the wisdom to teach the multitudes, the strength to confront spiritual opposition, the authority to heal broken bodies, and the love to care for the needy. Though Jesus spent countless hours serving others, He prioritized and carved out a sacred space in His heart and day where He met alone with His Father.

In the swift current of life, we, too, must reserve a sacred space to simply be with our God.

☼ *Being alone with God reminds us of His constant presence.*

☼ *Being still before God sensitizes us to His gentle guidance.*

☼ *Being silent before God strengthens us to speak His hope to a hurting world.*

RESTING IN
GOD'S PROVISION

~

WORDS FOR THE WORRIED

Therefore do not worry about tomorrow, for tomorrow will worry about itself. Each day has enough trouble of its own.
—MATTHEW 6:34

Jesus said, *"Do not worry about your life, what you will eat or drink; or about your body, what you will wear."* (Matt. 6:25)

This is not about caring, this is about fretting.

This is not about reasonable attention, this is about rising anxiety.

In our stress-saturated world, it is easy to justify worry. "It is not a lack of trust," we rationalize, "it is the presence of concern." But when "concern" begins to furrow our brow, tie knots in our stomach, incite us to nibble on our nails, interfere with our sleep, and cause us to forget that God is our Provider, we can call it what we want . . . but God calls it *worry*.

Worriers come in at least three levels of intensity. There

WORDS FOR THE WORRIED

is the Occasional Worrier who seems generally immune to anxiety except for one or two significant areas like finances or children or that odd pain in the back of the left ankle.

Then there are the Chronic (or constant) Worriers. Though busy, these worriers rarely celebrate the fruit of their labor. "Cannot spare the time," they think as they immediately reroute their worry from one resolved crisis to a new, worthy cause. In fact, Chronic Worriers never have a moment where their worry is not needed. They have causes and concerns lined up for years in advance.

Finally there are the Communal Worriers, who have more capacity for worry than their lives can soak up so they also worry for others. They even worry that others do not worry enough . . . which makes them more than a little vulnerable to nagging, but "at least they care enough to be concerned!"

In Matthew 6, Jesus identifies three principles that can help us win our war with worry.

1. Worry wastes time. It does not stop time.

Who of you by worrying can add a single hour to his life? (Matt. 6:27)

Time is one of our most precious resources, but worry spends it like a fool. Worry takes our time without adding anything to our lives—not an hour to our day, an inch to our height, or a penny to our pocket.

Suppose we all lived in a very dry region. Every day, we were given two gallons of water. We could (1) drink the water, (2) use it for cooking, (3) water our small gardens and grow food, or (4) pour it on the sidewalk or street. Most of us would choose some combination of numbers 1, 2, and 3. But worry is like choosing number 4.

Each day, we are given a finite amount of emotional energy. How will we spend it? Taking care of daily needs for living, wisely preparing for the future, or worrying about everything that could go wrong?

2. God knows what we need.

> Do not worry, saying, "What shall we eat?" or "What shall we drink?" or "What shall we wear?" For the pagans run after all these things, and your heavenly Father knows that you need them. (Matt. 6:31–32)

If God feeds the birds of the air and clothes the lilies of the field, He will certainly provide food and clothing for us. In every moment, God knows exactly what we truly need and what we truly want. He is a good Father who will not fail to take care of His children.

3. Seeking God is the wisest investment on earth.

Seek first his kingdom and his righteousness, and all these things will be given to you as well. (Matt. 6:33)

When we spend the best of our energy seeking God, we find ourselves sufficiently provided for in every area of our lives. We become less anxious about the temporal because focusing on knowing God keeps our perspective on the eternal.

Worry, on the other hand, is an unwise investment. It cannot sew cloths to dress us, cook a meal to feed us, or build a house to shelter us. All it does is burn up our limited supply of daily energy in the smoky fire of fear.

Whether we worry occasionally, chronically, or for the whole community, these principles from Jesus can strengthen us to invest our time wisely in following God instead of wasting our time foolishly in wearisome worry.

☼ *Worry spends time like a fool.*

☼ *Worry is a waste of energy because God already knows exactly what we need.*

☼ *Seeking God is the wisest investment of time on earth.*

CONTENTMENT

I can do everything through him who gives me strength.

—PHILIPPIANS 4:13

*C*ontentment cannot be bought. Most with little do not profess satisfaction, and many with much still want much more. "Having nothing" does not seem to free us from care any more than "having it all" guarantees fulfillment.

Craving, on the other hand, makes itself abundantly available. Countless times a day, our culture intentionally injects us with strong doses of dissatisfaction in an overt effort to make us discontent with *what is* and hungry for *what could be*. Millions of hours and untold dollars have been invested in research to discover what makes us, the consumer, crave. As we open the newspaper, go online, listen to the radio, or walk down the street our senses are bombarded by a continuous stream of persuasive suggestions that we need *something* more, *something* different, *something* better . . . and (lucky for us, or so the advertisers say) that *something* exists, "out there," only one purchase away.

So what does all this have to do with resting in God's provision? Unfortunately, a great deal because it forces upon us a serious question: When we pray to God for His provision, do we ask with a contented heart or a craving heart?

Do we believe that provision is the source of contentment? The apostle Paul did not.

Around A.D. 61, Paul wrote a letter to a church he had helped plant on his first missionary journey. Philippi was the Roman colony where Lydia first believed in Jesus, Paul and Silas were beaten and imprisoned for freeing a slave girl, and a jailer miraculously surrendered his life to God. Paul was a spiritual father to the Philippians. Let us listen to what Paul teaches them about the subject of contentment:

> *I rejoice greatly in the Lord that at last you have renewed your concern for me. Indeed, you have been concerned, but you had no opportunity to show it. I am not saying this because I am in need, for I have learned to be content whatever the circumstances.*

I know what it is to be in need, and I know what it is to have plenty. I have learned the secret of being content in any and every situation whether well fed or hungry, whether living in plenty or in want.

I can do everything through him who gives me strength. (Phil. 4:10–13)

What was Paul's secret to contentment? He makes it clear that it was not being *well-fed* or *hungry, living in plenty* or *in want.* In fact, Paul states that his contentment was totally unaffected by his circumstances.

Notably, Paul wrote these thoughts in a thank-you letter to a group that had sent him a missionary offering. He did not send the money back to the Philippian church with a note saying, "Return to sender. I am content." Being content did not mean that Paul no longer needed money or supplies. Paul kept the gift, wrote a thank-you, and in the thank-you explained that the money was helpful, he received it ·with gratitude, and its presence or absence had nothing to do with his contentment.

Why? Because the source of Paul's contentment was a Person, not provision. God gave him strength in every circumstance. With God by his side, Paul was satisfied.

So let us return to our question: Do we pray for God's provision with contented or craving hearts? Craving hearts will never know satisfaction regardless how often or how much God provides. But contented hearts always know satisfaction even before they finish their prayer.

※ *The source of true contentment is a Person, not provision.*

※ *With God by our side, we can be peaceful in any circumstance.*

※ *Contented hearts know satisfaction even before they finish their prayer.*

FACING A PROBLEM

"Where could we get enough bread in this remote place to feed such a crowd?"

—MATTHEW 15:33

Walking along the busy, oval shoreline of the Sea of Galilee, Jesus and His disciples slowly turned away from the waters toward the mountain. Passing shepherd and sheep, farmer and field, they eventually came upon an open space where they could sit and rest.

Throughout the decades to come, thousands would look with tears upon this very mountainside and remember the miracles that changed their lives. *There* the lame walked. *There* the blind could see. *There* the mute spoke. *There* the crippled were made whole.

There, for three entire days, the crowds laid the broken and needy at the feet of Jesus *"and he healed them."* (Matt. 15:30) Lame loved-ones went up the mountain carried on cots and came down the mountain dancing for joy. Blind children went up the mountain sitting on their parent's shoulders and came down the mountain stopping to marvel at each rock and bug. God was miraculously meeting the needs of His people.

On day three, Jesus began to hear a sound rising above the people's praises to God: the growling of over four thousand hungry stomachs!

> Jesus called his disciples to him and said, "I have compassion for these people; they have already been with me three days and have nothing to eat. I do not want to send them away hungry, or they may collapse on the way." His disciples answered, "Where could we get enough bread in this remote place to feed such a crowd?" (Matt. 15:32–33)

The disciples' response to Jesus reveals three stumbling blocks that we face in recognizing God's provision for our lives.

First, **the disciples failed to recall God's past faithfulness**. They could have said, "Well, in chapter fourteen, you blessed five loaves and two fish and multiplied them to feed over five thousand." But to the disciples, it was as though the events in chapter fourteen did not exist. They neither referenced nor remembered how God provided for them *last time*.

How easy it is for our memory of God's faithfulness to be erased by the loud grumbling of today's need. God provided for us in that crisis *last time*, but that was long ago . . . He gave us wisdom in a difficult situation *before*, but somehow this seems different . . .

When facing a problem, disciplining our minds to remember God's past faithfulness quiets our hearts to receive God's direction.

Secondly, **the disciples isolated God's current provision.** Perhaps Jesus' followers had amnesia about the last chapter, but they certainly could remember what they had seen that day! In front of their own eyes, Jesus had healed broken bodies and given sight to the blind.

Yet when Jesus asked them about providing food, they basically said, "Be realistic Jesus. We are on a remote mountainside." They had seen Him *heal* thousands, but in their minds *feeding* thousands was an entirely different matter.

Like the disciples, we often isolate God's provision to a specific area: "You helped me with my job, but I am not sure I can trust You with my family." Yet God's faithfulness is not finicky. He is faithful in ALL things!

When facing a problem, taking a personal inventory of God's current provision refreshes our confidence in God's character.

Third, **the disciples neglected to consider the size of their Source**. They surveyed the side of the mountain. They measured the density of the crowds. They examined the holes in their pockets. But they did not consider *Who* was drawing their attention to the problem.

Jesus cared about the need before the disciples saw the need. The same is true today. Jesus knows our concerns before we can even verbalize them.

When facing a problem, we can either choose to spend our time surveying the mountains, measuring the crowds, and examining the holes, or we can choose instead to consider the size of our Source. The first choice amplifies fear. The second choice applies faith.

☼ *Jesus cares about our needs before we even know our needs.*

☼ *When facing a problem, first consider the size and strength of your Source.*

☼ *We can be confident in God's character.*

LESSONS ON GOD'S PROVISION

And God provided. . . .
—JONAH 1:17

A nd God provided . . . a whale? A worm? A wind? Not quite what generally comes into our minds when we think of God's provision! But provision takes on different forms at different times . . . especially when we are running from God.

Consider God's provision in Jonah's life.

Jonah was from Gath Hepher, a town on the west side of the Sea of Galilee. He had the unusual ability to hear God's voice and then deliver God's messages to others. But one day, Jonah heard something he did not like:

The word of the LORD came to Jonah son of Amittai: "Go to the great city of Nineveh and preach against it, because its wickedness has come up before me." (Jonah 1:1–2)

Nineveh was a city of conquests and culture. The capital of ruling Assyria, Nineveh was surrounded by eight miles of brick walls that depicted her victories, history, and mythology. Rich gardens bordered her gates and priceless books filled her library. She was sophisticated, politically unmatched, and spiritually lost. In Jonah's day there were over 120,000 people in Nineveh who could not, *"tell their right hand from their left."* (Jonah 4:11)

So God commissioned a prophet to Nineveh to call them to repentance, but the prophet did not want to go. The Assyrians were a threat to Jonah's people and he had no desire to show mercy to his enemies. Instead of traveling northeast toward Nineveh, Jonah went southwest and boarded a ship headed in the opposite direction:

> *But Jonah ran away from the LORD and headed for Tarshish. He went down to Joppa, where he found a ship bound for that port. After paying the fare, he went aboard and sailed for Tarshish to flee from the LORD.* (Jonah 1:3)

Jonah told the crew that *"he was running away from the LORD."* But they did not pay much attention to his confession until a violent storm threatened their lives. At Jonah's urging, they dumped the honest, rebellious prophet overboard and the seas became like glass.

Then, *"the* LORD *provided a great fish to swallow Jonah, and Jonah was inside the fish three days and three nights."* (Jonah 1:17)

Have you ever found yourself stuck in a smelly, murky mess? Before we ask God for a way out, it would be wise for us to ask God how we got in. Sometimes God provides a great fish to save us from ourselves.

Jonah recognized that he was disobeying God. This was not deception, this was rebellion. The whale was Jonah's last opportunity to repent.

We know the story well: Jonah prayed . . . God heard . . . the whale suffered indigestion . . . God spoke again . . . Jonah went to Nineveh . . . the people turned from their sin . . . and the pouting prophet found a spot to sit and wait for God to change His mind and destroy the city.

Nineveh was repentant but God's prophet was still in sin. God had provided a whale to address his rebellion, now He provided a vine, worm, and wind to address his utter lack of compassion.

While hatred, anger, and revenge ate their way through Jonah's soul, a worm ate its way through Jonah's shade tree. When the tree withered and the hot winds scorched him, Jonah told God, *"I am angry enough to die."* (Jonah 4:9) God took that moment to try to show the prophet His concern for the city of Nineveh and Jonah's absolute lack of love for anyone but himself.

And then—well, the story stops. Jonah told others his story (in fact, Jesus referred to it more than once) but we do not know if the prophet changed his heart.

So, what about our hearts? Have we, like Jonah, known God's will but headed in the opposite direction? Have we, like Jonah, underestimated the price we could ultimately pay for willful disobedience? If so, in God's mercy we will soon see, and feel, His provision.

What will we do when God provides a whale or a worm or a wind? How will we respond when our comforts are removed and our circumstances start to stink? God's provision can take on less than welcome shapes. But all of His provision is given for our eternal good.

- ☼ *When stuck in the muck, it would be wise to ask God how we got there.*

- ☼ *Sometimes God provides a "great fish" to save us from ourselves.*

- ☼ *That painful form of provision may be our last chance to repent.*

LOVING LIMITS

LORD, you have assigned me my portion and my cup; you have made my lot secure. The boundary lines have fallen for me in pleasant places; surely I have a delightful inheritance.
—PSALM 16:5–6

Assigned portions and cups. Secured lots. Lined boundaries. The psalmist viewed these thoughts as *pleasant* and *delightful*. But we do not necessarily share his opinion today.

Limits in general have fallen into disrepute. If they must exist, portions should be self-designated and ever-expanding. Unless marking off land, boundaries should be flexible or altogether absent (after all, the very word cramps our creativity). And lines can be useful if viewed as erasable suggestions.

Ages ago, one man held a drastically different perspective. In Psalm 16:5–6, David rejoiced that his portions were *not* self-assigned. He was grateful that God had established his boundaries. He saw lines as peace-inspiring reminders of God's provision in his life.

God, not David, had designated his portions. God, not fate, had secured his lot in life. God, not man, had appointed his inheritance. These realizations filled David with joy, not regret; with security, not restlessness.

Yet today, we often feel confined and offended by the thought of anyone else, including God, appointing our portions or selecting our boundaries. God is welcome to offer opinions but making decisions is another matter.

We want to be the masters of our own destiny, thank you. Independence is the road to fulfillment, we say. Self-determination is the door to enlightenment, we boast. After all, look how far they have brought us . . .

Indeed, look how far they have brought us.

We designate our own portions, and eat too much. We establish our own boundaries, and take on too much. We attempt to secure our own lots, and worry ourselves into exhaustion.

Perhaps we could use some help.

David found that help in God. He realized that submission to God's plans expanded—as opposed to hindered—his life. God's boundaries caused him to flourish, not flounder. He thrived when God was in charge.

David loved limits that were established by his God.

Why? Because he trusted Him.

And maybe trust is our true challenge.

We ask God to provide for us, but do we trust Him to decide what and how much we really need? In a day where we celebrate "no limits," dare we invite God to establish limits in our lives?

Frankly, if we have risked trusting ourselves, it should be easy to trust God. He has a much better record of faithfulness than we do. God has never overcommitted or under-delivered. He has never been motivated by selfish ambition or greed. He is just and generous, wise and patient.

God knows the future and understands our past. In every moment, He fully comprehends what is best for us. God will not over-feed, over-extend, or give us more than is good for our souls. His leadership is faultless. The plans He has appointed for us are good. God offers to set aside sufficient provision for us. He longs to designate loving boundaries that will make our lives secure.

If God is not worthy of our trust, who is?

Lasting fulfillment is the fruit of active God-dependence, not of striving self-direction. Peace-filled provision awaits those who join David in risking the path of willful surrender to God!

☀ *We thrive when God is in charge.*

☀ *God's trustworthy boundaries are empowering, not confining.*

☀ *Surrendering to God produces a harvest of peace.*

THE SAVIOR HAS COME!

He found the place where it is written: "The Spirit of the LORD is on me."

—LUKE 4:17–18

Nestled around the base of a hill, the town of Nazareth slept peacefully between the Sea of Galilee and the Mediterranean. The agricultural community was small, filled with fewer than two-thousand souls, and happily just outside of the traffic-laden trade routes.

Others underestimated and even mocked Nazareth. But as the sun rose, little did the city know that today she would underestimate and mock God's Messiah.

"I'm ready father," said Janen.

"So soon? When have I seen my son so anxious to go to synagogue?" Janen's father asked with a grin.

Janen bit his lip pensively then decided to speak, "Rumor is that Joseph's son will be there today. Do you think—could he be a prophet, or maybe even more?"

"Ah! Someone has been listening to the stories in the market. Seems like Jesus has become a good teacher, and

THE SAVIOR HAS COME!

we are proud of him. But a prophet? Not likely my son."

The reading of the *Shema*ʿ, the reciting of prayers, the reading from the Law . . . then Janen held his breath as the leader called upon the carpenter's son to read from the Prophets.

Jesus stood, unrolled the scroll, and read,

> *"The Spirit of the LORD is on me, because he has anointed me to preach good news to the poor. He has sent me to proclaim freedom for the prisoners and recovery of sight for the blind, to release the oppressed, to proclaim the year of the LORD's favor."* (Luke 4:18–19)

Isaiah's prophecy about the coming of God's Chosen One? Could it be that my eyes will see the day of . . .— Janen dared not finish the thought. The room was still as Jesus sat down to expound the Scriptures. His authority was felt even without words. But then he spoke, *"Today this scripture is fulfilled in your hearing."* (Luke 4:21)

In the brief silence that followed, the weight of Jesus' announcement fell upon the unsuspecting town. In a few hungry hearts like Janen's, Jesus' messianic claim inspired faith. But for most that day, Jesus' declaration was met with rage. Before the sun set, Nazareth had seen, heard, rejected, and attempted to kill God's Chosen One.

But let us sit for a few moments longer with Janen. He had listened to Isaiah's messianic prophecy many times before. But imagine hearing these words from the mouth of the Savior. What had Jesus, the Messiah, come to provide?

I, your Messiah, have come. The Spirit has anointed me to preach good news to the poor. The Greek word *euangelizō*, here translated *preach good news,* is used in the New Testament to describe telling, bringing, or announcing the glad news of God's salvation. Jesus came to provide us— the lowly, the destitute, the helpless, the physically and spiritually needy—with eternal encouragement.

I, your Messiah, have come. God sent me to proclaim freedom for the prisoners. Only here does the Greek work *aphesis* appear as *freedom.* Most often it is translated *forgiveness.* Jesus came to provide us—those who have been imprisoned and held captive by our sins—with cleansing for our souls.

I, your Messiah, have come. I am here to bring sight to the blind. The word translated *blind* is elsewhere used to refer to physical, mental, and spiritual blindness. Jesus came to provide us—who know darkness of the body, mind, or heart—with vision from Him.

I, your Messiah, have come. I am here to release the oppressed. The word translated *oppressed* means *to break into pieces.* Jesus came to provide us—the shattered and bruised—with freedom from our brokenness.

I, your Messiah, have come. I proclaim to you that this is the year of the Lord's favor. In this, Janen would have heard Jesus say, "The long awaited day of the Messiah has come to you. This is the year of the Lord's acceptance." And with those words, an invitation would have sounded in his heart: "Do I believe? Will I receive God's Messiah?"

That invitation echoes through the ages to sound in our hearts today. Will we believe? Will we receive God's Messiah?

Jesus, the Savior, has come to provide us—the poor, needy, imprisoned, blind, and broken—with eternal encouragement, spiritual cleansing, light, and freedom for our souls! Will we believe?

☼ *Jesus, our Messiah, has come!*

☼ *Jesus has the authority to free captives from sin and to mend the broken in spirit.*

☼ *The good news of God provides undying hope for our hearts.*

RESTING IN
GOD'S LOVE

〜〜

A CHILD LEADS US THERE

"Let the little children come to me."

—MARK 10:14

"Teacher, let your blessing rest on my boy."

"Jesus, would you pray for my child?"

"Rabbi, please place your hands upon my baby."

People were bringing little children to Jesus to have Him touch them, but the disciples disapproved. Perhaps they assumed Jesus was too busy or too important. Maybe they thought the children were a distraction or simply insignificant.

"Leave the Teacher alone," the disciples said rebuking the parents, certain that Jesus did not wish to be bothered by a child's desire for affection or a parent's request for blessing.

They were severely wrong: *"When Jesus saw this, he was indignant."* (Mark 10:14) The Greek *aganakteō* here translated *indignant* means to be grieved or to feel much pain. Seeing the children sent away literally hurt Jesus' heart.

He said to them, "Let the little children come to me, and do not hinder them, for the kingdom of God belongs to such as these. I tell you the truth, anyone who will not receive the kingdom of God like a little child will never enter it."

And he took the children in his arms, put his hands on them and blessed them. (Mark 10:14–16)

At Jesus' invitation, the children came running. The little girl with long black curls skipped into His arms while a shy three-year-old quietly peaked around His shoulder. The tough toddler with dirt on his shirt climbed up onto Jesus' knee and a bright young boy gently sat at His feet. Jesus opened His arms, received each one, and placed His hand of blessing upon them. And it is safe to assume that He smiled.

In this interaction, Jesus publicly corrected His disciples for hindering children from coming to Him. He even suggested that His leaders-in-training should see the children as their teachers. Something in their actions had revealed a key to receiving the kingdom of God.

Perhaps part of that key was the children's lack of self-consciousness in coming to Jesus. It did not occur to them to withhold their affections because of social expectations. They sensed His love and sought His touch.

When was the last time we responded to God's love unhindered by self-consciousness? At what age did we decide we were too old to seek His touch? Somewhere, somehow we began to believe that to ask is to need, to need is to be weak, to be weak is to be vulnerable, and to be vulnerable is to be hurt.

Children do not accept these flawed, self-protective assumptions. Without shame they make their need for affection known. "I want to be with you," they declare loudly without embarrassment or apology. "Hold me!" they request boldly with their arms confidently lifted in the air.

God longs for the same child-like affection from us. He longs for us to press past the suffocating layers of faulty thinking that encourage us to "not bother God" with a simple request for His touch.

When we run into His open arms of love, without shame or apology, we move one step closer to the kingdom of God.

(And it is still safe to assume that God smiles.)

☼ *God longs for us to seek His touch.*

☼ *To do so freely, we must abandon our self-protective defenses and self-conscious cautions.*

☼ *When we approach Jesus with child-like love, His arms open wide to receive us!*

A MIGHTY SHOUT
FROM HEAVEN

*How great is the love the Father has lavished on us, that we
should be called children of God! And that is what we are!*
—1 JOHN 3:1

Why does Father God love us?

Is it because of our goodness? Doubtful. We know what is in our hearts.

Is it because of our brilliance? Ridiculous. Compared with His wisdom, only the deluded could boast.

Is it because of our abilities? Hardly. Why would the Creator of the Universe be impressed with our talents?

Then if not for our hearts, heads, or hands, why does God love us? Perhaps we will find answers when we consider the Father's great love for Jesus.

We actually know very little about most of Jesus' earthly life. Apart from His baby dedication, the Magi's visit, and His brief adventure in the temple at the age of twelve, enormous gaps of silence exist between Jesus' famous birth and the beginning of His adult ministry.

After thirty mostly hidden years, Jesus journeyed *"from Galilee to the Jordan to be baptized by John. But John tried to deter him, saying, 'I need to be baptized by you, and do you come to me?' Jesus replied, 'Let it be so now.'"* (Matt. 3:13–15)

Consenting to Jesus' request, John immersed Jesus in the waters and the miraculous occurred: *"As soon as Jesus was baptized, he went up out of the water. At that moment heaven was opened, and he saw the Spirit of God descending like a dove and lighting on him."* (Matt. 3:16)

As Jesus emerged from the water, the sky split open! The Holy Spirit in the form of a dove gently descended from heaven and remained on Him. Then, *"A voice from heaven said, 'This is my Son, whom I love; with him I am well pleased.'"* (Matt. 3:17)

As the Holy Spirit rested upon Jesus, He heard an audible sound (*phōnē*) emanating from the open sky. Father God had something He wanted to say: "I dearly love you Son! I am so pleased with who you are!"

Quite a production to say "I love you."

Significantly, Father God shouts this affirmation before Jesus saves one soul or preaches one sermon. Father God proclaims His love for Jesus before He heals one body or casts out one demon. This affirmation is spoken over Jesus not as an amazing teacher or miracle-worker or even coming Messiah. Father God shouts His love over Jesus *as His Son*.

Why does God love us? For the same reason He loves Jesus, because we are His children!

From the heavens He says, "I love you son! I love you daughter!" His voice is not louder when we are successful and silent when we fail. His cry is not prouder when we are strong and muffled when we are weak. Nor is God withholding this affirmation until we accomplish something great or discover something new.

Today, wherever we are, whatever we have or have not achieved, God is still shouting His message of love. The heavens may not split and a dove may not descend, but Father God's voice is still shouting: "Know that I dearly love you child, simply because you are Mine!"

☼ *God loves us because we are* His.

☼ *His love does not increase or decrease based on our accomplishments.*

☼ *Whether we are hidden or applauded, Father God shouts over us, "My child, I dearly love you!"*

DIRTY FEET, CLEANSED HEARTS

He . . . showed them the full extent of his love.

—JOHN 13:1

Not by healing. Not with answers. Not through miracles. Not with words . . . Jesus demonstrated "the full extent of His love" by washing the disciple's feet.

The Passover meal was being served and Judas had already decided to betray Jesus. Jesus knew that very soon the disciples would desert Him and He would enter into the final torturous hours of His life on earth.

Looking around the table at Judas the betrayer, Peter the denier, and ten other deserters, most of us would *not* be thinking, "I really love these guys!"

But Jesus was. Human weakness did not dilute the strength of His love.

So He rose from the table and shed His tunic. The Twelve were no doubt curious, but by now they had learned to expect the unexpected with Jesus. However, when Jesus wrapped a towel around His waist and poured water in a basin they began to feel uncomfortable.

The gospel of Luke records that earlier in the meal there had been a dispute among the disciples. Jesus had taken the cup and bread, given thanks, and through these elements illustrated His coming sacrifice for the sins of the world. Immediately following this powerful visual of His provision for forgiveness, He mentioned that one of the Twelve would betray Him.

Instead of meditating on what Jesus was trying to communicate through the Passover symbols or soberly considering their own capacity for sin, the disciples tried to figure out which one of them would become the betrayer. Their method was the process of elimination: eliminate from the list of suspects whoever was *the greatest*. They seemed to believe that spiritual experiences and gifting somehow immunized them from failure.

The talk around the table might have sounded something like this:

John: "Well, the betrayer obviously can't be me, James, or Peter. Jesus chose us to be with Him during His transfiguration. The rest of you were waiting at the base of the mountain and together you couldn't even heal that small boy."

Phillip: "What?! You think you're the greatest? At

least we weren't the ones Jesus rebuked for wanting to call down fire from heaven on that city!"

Thomas: "Or the one who almost drowned trying to walk on water . . ."

Peter: "Hey, at least I had the faith to get out of the boat!"

In the shadow of this rather ugly debate, Jesus dresses like a servant, kneels down, and starts washing the disciples' dirty, calloused feet. Those who, moments before, had been boasting about their greatness were now looking for a way to hide their less-than-great feet from the eyes and hands of Jesus.

Scripture states that in this act Jesus "showed them the full extent of His love." So what lessons of love can we learn two thousand years later as we watch Jesus wash the disciple's feet?

God's love extends to us, even when we are about to fail Him. Jesus washed all the disciple's feet: those of the betrayer, the denier, and the deserters. His love *for us* is not decreased by the sin *in us*.

God's love is strengthened, not weakened, by service. Jesus did not become less by giving more. The evidence of His love in our lives is internal humility, not external greatness.

God's love is not squeamish. It voluntarily handles the least presentable parts of our lives. The last thing we want God to see in us is the first thing He kneels down to touch with His strong healing hands.

The most convincing proof of God's love towards us is found in His cleansing, not in His giftings. Jesus showed His love for the Twelve not by giving them gifts or increasing their abilities or endowing them with more authority but by washing them clean.

We need look no further than our own dirty feet and cleansed hearts to begin each morning confident of God's love for us!

- *Our human weakness does not dilute the strength of God's love.*

- *Jesus demonstrated His love by cleansing betrayers, deniers, and deserters alike.*

- *God is willing to touch and purify even the most embarrassing parts of our lives.*

THE CROSS

For God so loved the world that he gave his one and only
Son, that whoever believes in him shall not perish but have
eternal life.

—JOHN 3:16

Rarely do we find a cross in a church that even remotely resembles the cross of Jesus Christ. They seem to be lacking in splinters and blood. Our modern crosses are made of precious metals and polished to perfection. Symmetrical and spotless, we mount them under adoring lights or poise them atop spiraling steeples.

So it is understandable that the sight of such crosses does not bring us to our knees in gratitude to God. Understandable . . . but unfortunate. Jesus' cross would have made us weep.

It was rough and rugged and merciless. It represented humiliation and rejection and failure. It tore His flesh and absorbed His blood. And through it we now know the love of God.

We cannot rest in God's love without remembering

Christ's cross. The two are bound together, dependant on and reflective of each other. The blood-stained cross of Jesus is the clearest and most compelling evidence of God's great love for us.

Consider what the writers of the New Testament said about the connection between Jesus' sacrifice and the love of God:

You see, at just the right time, when we were still powerless, Christ died for the ungodly. Very rarely will anyone die for a righteous man, though for a good man someone might possibly dare to die. But God demonstrates his own love for us in this: While we were still sinners, Christ died for us. (Rom. 5:6–8)

When we were weak and unable to help ourselves, Jesus came to our rescue. With no guarantee that we would even care, Jesus died for us. He submitted to the cross—a punishment normally reserved for the lowest of criminals—so that sinners could experience God's love.

Because of his great love for us, God, who is rich in mercy, made us alive with Christ even when we were dead in transgressions—it is by grace you have been saved. . . . Christ loved us and gave himself up for us as a fragrant offering and sacrifice to God. (Eph. 2:4–5; 5:2)

When we were spiritually lifeless because of our sins, Jesus sacrificed Himself to save us. In His rich and surpassing love, Jesus laid down His life through a humiliating death—one that the religious viewed as cursed—so that we could be become alive in Him.

This is how God showed his love among us: He sent his one and only Son into the world that we might live through him. This is love: not that we loved God, but that he loved us and sent his Son as an atoning sacrifice for our sins. (1 John 4:9–10)

Even when we were loveless toward God, He sent His Son as evidence of His unfathomable love for us. Jesus embraced unimaginable pain—through one of the cruelest forms of execution known to man—so that we could live for God.

When we were powerless, ungodly, and unrighteous, dead in our transgressions, and without love for God, Jesus died on the cross to save us!

Now that is love. That is worth living for. That is even worth dying for. And that is most definitely worth resting in!

☼ *We cannot rest in God's love without remembering Christ's cross.*

☼ *Without the cross, we would still be powerless and dead in our sins.*

☼ *The bloodstained cross of Jesus is the most compelling evidence of God's great love for us.*

TESTS OF TRUE LOVE

God is love. Whoever lives in love lives in God, and God in him.

—1 JOHN 4:16

ove was not the first word that came to people's minds when they thought of John, the son of Zebedee. His temper and aggressive personality had given him a somewhat less than loving reputation. But Jesus is not intimidated by fiery emotions. John and his brother James were among the first disciples Jesus called to Himself; He referred to the pair as "Sons of Thunder."

They lived up to their name!

As a young man, John was assertively elitist: *"Teacher," said John, "we saw a man driving out demons in your name and we told him to stop, because he was not one of us."* (Mark 9:38)

He was impatient and judgmental: *But the people there did not welcome him, because he was heading for Jerusalem. When the disciples James and John saw this, they asked, "Lord, do you want us to call fire down from heaven to destroy them?" But Jesus turned and rebuked them.* (Luke 9:53–55)

And he was unashamedly ambitious: *Then James and John, the sons of Zebedee, came to him. "Teacher" they said, "we want you to do for us whatever we ask. . . . Let one of us sit at your right and the other at your left in your glory."* (Mark 10:35, 37)

But his three-year mentoring relationship with Jesus evidently included a life-changing course on anger management because the disciple once called "Son of Thunder" is known to us today as the "Apostle of Love."

At least fifty years after Jesus' resurrection, John wrote a letter to the churches of Asia Minor. One of the primary themes of this first epistle was love. In fact the word *love* makes over forty appearances in 1 John. So it is to John we now turn for insight into how we can know that God's love is truly growing within us.

John teaches that the love of God dwells in us if . . .

We obey God's Word. *"If anyone obeys his word, God's love is truly made complete in him.* (1 John 2:5) No trades are permitted here. There is nothing we can offer God that can substitute for obedience as proof of His love in us. If we love Him, we will endeavor to obey Him.

We do not love the world. *"If anyone loves the world, the love of the Father is not in him. For everything in the world—the cravings of sinful man, the lust of his eyes and the* *boasting of what he has and does—comes not from the Father but from the world."* (1 John 2:15–16) It is not possible for us to simultaneously pledge our allegiance to the world's lusts and God's love. To believe otherwise is to live as a deceived citizen in the kingdom of darkness. As God's love grows within us, love for the world begins to wither and die.

We are generous to those in need. *"If anyone has material possessions and sees his brother in need but has no pity on him, how can the love of God be in him? Dear children, let us not love with words or tongue but with actions and in truth."* (1 John 3:17–18) God's love cultivates compassion in our hearts. John teaches us that the test of love is not simply feeling compassionate but actively being generous towards others in need.

We love each other. *"If we love one another, God lives in us and his love is made complete in us."* (1 John 4:12) Throughout his letter, John repeatedly calls us to love each other. For him, the truest test of our love for God is our love for one another. John makes it clear: If we nurture hatred for our brothers and sisters in Christ, we cannot love or even really know God. (1 John 4:8, 20–21)

Had John been an innately gentle soul, we might be able to dismiss his emphasis on God's love as a mere reflection of his personality. But for John, love did not come naturally. The love we see demonstrated in 1 John is the fruit of fifty years of following God. How encouraging for all who wrestle with hot tempers and short fuses! God is still transforming sons and daughters of thunder into teachers of love.

- ☼ *Walking with Jesus quiets the angry and impatient thunder in our personalities.*

- ☼ *The evidence of God's love in our lives is obedience to His Word.*

- ☼ *God's love gains strength within us as we are generous and loving toward one another.*

LOVE'S BACKBONE

The Lord disciplines those he loves.

—HEBREWS 12:6

ove. Rest in God's love. And while we are resting . . . let us remember that discipline is not the antonym of love, discipline is the backbone of love. Without discipline, love is spineless.

The two greatest concentrations of teaching on discipline in the Bible are found in Proverbs and Hebrews. In Proverbs, the Hebrew word most often translated discipline, *mûsar*, appears eighteen times, primarily in the teachings of Solomon. Scripture tells us that, *"All the kings of the earth sought audience with Solomon to hear the wisdom God had put in his heart."* (2 Chron. 9:23) So what did the wisest sage on the planet have to say about God's discipline?

> *He who heeds discipline shows the way to life, but whoever ignores correction leads others astray.* (Prov. 10:17)
> *Whoever loves discipline loves knowledge, but*

> *he who hates correction is stupid.* (Prov. 12:1)
> *He who ignores discipline despises himself,*
> *but whoever heeds correction gains understanding.*
> (Prov. 15:32)

Since we do not want to be foolish, lead others astray, or otherwise despise ourselves we somehow need to adopt Solomon's attitude and begin viewing the discipline of God as a welcome, wisdom-producing, life-giving gift.

This is certainly how the writer of Hebrews viewed God's discipline. In his teaching on the subject he quotes Solomon's wisdom from Proverbs 3:11–12:

> *My son, do not make light of the Lord's disci-*
> *pline, and do not lose heart when he rebukes you,*
> *because the Lord disciplines those he loves, and*
> *he punishes everyone he accepts as a son.* (Heb.
> 12:5–6)

The Greek word used in Hebrews to speak of discipline, *paideuō*, means *to train* or *instruction*. The concept specifically relates to raising children; in fact, it is from this Greek word that the English word *pedagogy* (the art or profession of teaching) is derived.

Drawing from the wisdom of Proverbs and Hebrews, a working definition of God's discipline could be "loving but painful instruction." The presence of God's discipline is actually an encouraging reminder of His Fatherhood in our lives. As with any earthly parent, God's discipline seems to take on many forms: post-sin punishment, mid-sin rebuke, pre-sin preventative instruction, and no-sin hardship.

Punishment connects choice with consequence. In Hebrews 12:6 we learn that God *"punishes everyone he accepts as a son."* To help us learn from (as opposed to repeat) our errors, God allows us to experience consequences from our sin. Always rescuing others from the effects of their choices is not love, it is sabotage.

Rebuke as it appears in Hebrews 12:5, *elenchō,* is elsewhere translated *expose, convict,* and *correct.* God's rebuke stings but it is generally still less painful than His punishment. Rebuke stops us from continuing on a harmful path in our thoughts or actions. When heeded, God's rebuke brings life and wisdom.

Preventative instruction is normally our preference among these four types of discipline. Here God assumes the role of loving Teacher, and we gladly assume the posture of hungry student. As with all good teachers, God clearly communicates principles of truth to us through His Word. And like all good students, sometimes words are simply not enough!

This leads us to a fourth form of God's discipline: no-sin hardship. The writer of Hebrews instructs us to, *"Endure hardship as discipline; God is treating you as sons. For what son is not disciplined by his father?"* (Heb. 12:7) *Endure hardship* is translated from the Greek *hypomenō*, which means *to stay behind, to stand still, to take patiently.* Here it refers to remaining under unfortunate circumstances and trials. Significantly, this encouragement follows the writer's teaching on the hardships of those listed in the Hall of Faith in Hebrews chapter eleven. For them, and for us, God allows hardships to develop godly character.

Whether through punishment, rebuke, instruction, or hardship, the writer of Hebrews goes on to assure us that,

> God disciplines us for our good, that we may share in his holiness. No discipline seems pleasant at the time, but painful. Later on, however, it produces a harvest of righteousness and peace for those who have been trained by it. (Heb. 12:10–11)

So as we rest in God's love, let us also rejoice in His discipline. Without discipline, God's love would be mere sentiment. Without love, His discipline would be impossible to bear. Together, they mark us as God's children and keep us on His path.

☼ *God's love is not spineless: He disciplines those He loves for their good.*

☼ *Rebuke, instruction, and hardship are reminders that God is treating us as dearly loved children.*

☼ *When heeded, God's discipline is a wisdom-giving, peace-producing gift.*

RESTING IN
GOD'S FORGIVENESS

EXTRAVAGANT!

Wash me, and I will be whiter than snow.

—PSALM 51:7

Layers of sin had completely soiled his soul.

A spoiled king—he had the world but wanted more.

A heartless thief—he took from those with little
and left them with nothing.

An abusive leader—he used his God-given authority
to fulfill his self-serving plans.

An adulterer—he slept with and impregnated
another man's wife.

A manipulator—he sought to conceal the evidence
with deception.

A murderer—he buried his evil in an innocent
man's grave.

King David was a sinner, *just like us*. We too have been
greedy and unfair. We too have murdered others with our
words. We too have taken without pity. We too have
lusted and deceived.

We too, like David, can have our soiled souls washed whiter than snow!

David's heart was dripping with unfaithfulness to his crown, his leaders, his people, his family, and ultimately his God. But when Nathan the prophet confronted him, David earnestly repented:

> *David said to Nathan, "I have sinned against the LORD." Nathan replied, "The LORD has taken away your sin. You are not going to die. But because by doing this you have made the enemies of the LORD show utter contempt, the son born to you will die." (2 Sam. 12:13–14)*

David sinned severely and repented sincerely. He was forgiven by God, and he grieved over the consequences of his sin. But that is not the end of the story.

> *Then David comforted his wife Bathsheba, and he went to her and lay with her. She gave birth to a son, and they named him Solomon. The LORD loved him; and because the LORD loved him, he sent word through Nathan the prophet to name him Jedidiah. (2 Sam. 12:24–25)*

Consider how absolutely extravagant God's forgiveness is in David's life. Not only does He purify David's dirty soul, He blesses this formerly adulterous relationship with another child. Then, to set David and Bathsheba's heart at rest, God sends Nathan the prophet back to David to name the child Jedidiah, which means *beloved of Jehovah*!

Their son, Solomon, is surely one of richest symbols of God's unfathomable mercy. Of all David's sons, God chose Solomon to succeed him as king. Then God gifted Solomon with wisdom beyond measure. His writings are included in the Bible, and his name appears in Matthew's genealogy of Jesus.

"Wash me and I will be whiter than snow," was not wishful thinking on David's part. *"Create in me a pure heart,"* was not a prosaic illusion. These words describe reality for all who are sincerely repentant. God washes us whiter than snow. God creates in us a pure heart.

After failures, many of us spend days and years hanging our heads in shame, certain that God is now embarrassed by us. But God does not forgive us grudgingly. He is not stingy with His mercy. His love is not lost when we fall. God's forgiveness is gladly given and thoroughly complete.

David no doubt remembered this thorough, complete forgiveness of God every time he saw his precious son. Perhaps watching Solomon grow under the grudge-free blessing of God prompted him to write later in his life,

> *He does not treat us as our sins deserve or repay us according to our iniquities. For as high as the heavens are above the earth, so great is his love for those who fear him; as far as the east is from the west, so far has he removed our transgressions from us.* (Ps. 103:10–12)

True. How wonderfully true!

☀ *God's extravagant forgiveness washes repentant souls whiter than snow!*

☀ *When we repent sincerely, God forgives us fully.*

☀ *God's forgiveness is extravagant!*

WILL WE FORGIVE?

If we confess our sins, he is faithful and just and will forgive us our sins and purify us from all unrighteousness.

—1 JOHN 1:9

Yes, God is faithful to forgive us our sins. But how can we truly forgive ourselves?

Many live with the shame of personal failure. Deception, unfaithfulness, slander, impurity, abusiveness, jealousy, lies . . . these sins haunt us like shadows. But for some, these shadows are not unwelcome. God has forgiven us but we cannot imagine forgiving ourselves: "He is gracious to offer, but we do not deserve to receive."

How can we journey from failure to forgiveness? Let us learn from Peter's experience as one who denied His Lord.

Remember that Jesus knew. During a dinner with the Twelve, Jesus revealed that one of them would betray Him and all of them would fall away. The stunned disciples were speechless, except for Peter:

Peter replied, "Even if all fall away on account of you, I never will." Jesus answered, "I tell you the truth, this very night, before the rooster crows, you will disown me three times." (Matt. 26:33–34)

Though our hearts sometimes feel like strangers to us, they are entirely known to God. Our failures do not shock Him. In the shadow of sin, we must remember that Jesus knew we would fall before we knew we could fall.

Remember that Jesus saw. After the guards arrested Jesus, they took Him to the high priest's home. Peter followed at a distance and then entered the courtyard to warm himself by the fire. There, just as Jesus had predicted, Peter began to deny all knowledge of His Lord. At the very moment of Peter's third denial, *"the rooster crowed. The Lord turned and looked straight at Peter."* (Luke 22:60–61)

Though it may seem too painful to bear, we must accept the reality that Jesus saw us in our exact moment of failure. He was there, looking into our eyes as we chose the path of sin. Let us hold that piercing truth in our hearts as we consider another lesson from Peter's life.

Remember that Jesus died. With the memory of Jesus' gaze burning in his mind, Peter runs out of the

SITTING IN GOD'S SUNSHINE

courtyard weeping bitterly. His failure was undeniable and Jesus' eyes would prove unforgettable. His face swollen with tears, his heart bleeding from within, Peter joined the others as they watched in utter helplessness the brutal crucifixion of their Lord. Then from the cross, Peter heard these words: *"Father, forgive them, for they do not know what they are doing."* (Luke 23:34)

We, too, need to hear Jesus speak these words over our failures. There, on the cross, Jesus died for EVERY sin that we would ever commit. See Him die. Consider His pain. And then try to tell Him that His sufferings were simply not enough. Try to explain to Jesus that even though He paid for your sins with His death, you still need to pay for your sins in your life.

Die to your own pride and humbly heed His call. The disciples placed Jesus' body in a rock tomb and returned to their homes to keep the Sabbath. As soon as the sun rose on the first day of the week, Mary Magdalene, Mary the mother of James, and Salome returned to the tomb to find a moved stone and shiny angel:

> *"You are looking for Jesus the Nazarene, who was crucified. He has risen! He is not here. See the place where they laid him. But go, tell his disci-*

*ples **and Peter**, 'He is going ahead of you into Galilee. There you will see him, just as he told you.'"* (Mark 16:6–8)

To punish ourselves with unforgiveness is to place distance between us and our Forgiver. Jesus seems to address this distance when—through an angel then through the women—He specifically called Peter to come meet with Him again.

We, too, hear this call from Jesus. Perhaps through a child's prayer or a pastor's message, a friend's encouragement, or even the pages of this book, Jesus invites us to come near Him again. Only pride, clothed in self-pity or self-punishment, could refuse such an invitation.

Though broken and utterly disappointed in himself, Peter did not refuse Jesus' invitation.

Will we?

☼ *Jesus knew when we would sin before we knew we could sin.*

☼ *From the cross, He saw our exact moment of failure.*

☼ *Jesus paid the full price for our sins. Only pride could believe that His sacrifice is simply not enough.*

LEFTOVERS . . . AGAIN

If you forgive men when they sin against you, your
heavenly Father will also forgive you.

—MATTHEW 6:14

eftovers . . . again! How much of dish did we make? And why? Were we planning on feeding the planet?! It seems like there will never be an end to this dish!

No, this is not about the century-old fruitcake from Great Aunt Petunia or that earthy neighbor's tofu meatloaf. Neither is this bald cousin Harry's triple-fried-chicken or our own energy-producing five-bean chili. This addictive leftover is the ultimate classic: Have you ever served yourself *rehash of the past*?

Somewhere, somehow, someone hurt us and we have kept that wound in our active memory, pressing rewind and play in the theatre of our minds. With each rehearsal, we see it all and feel it all and digest it all over again.

Countless times we have taken our official last bite, decided to throw the rest out, and then—driven by some inner compulsion—we return to serve ourselves yet another helping.

Jesus tells us that this leftover is lethal: *"If you forgive men when they sin against you, your heavenly Father will also forgive you. But if you do not forgive men their sins, neither will your Father forgive your sins."* (Matt. 6:14–15)

In this passage, *sins* refers to offences, faults, stumbling, and errors. Jesus is calling us to *forgive* other's failings. *Forgive* is from a Greek word that is more often translated *leave* or *left*. This is how the word appears a few chapters earlier to describe Peter and Andrew's response to Jesus: *"They immediately **left** their nets and followed Him."* (Matt. 4:20, NKJV) To forgive is to leave it behind, to not bring it with you, to abandon it, to dismiss it, to *let it go*.

Forgiving means that, like these early disciples, we abandon our "nets" of bitterness so we can follow Jesus freely. Forgiving means we stop pressing rewind and play. Forgiving means we refuse to let our minds house the moldy leftovers of other's sins against us.

Jesus makes it clear: *rehash of the past* is a spiritual poison that hinders us from receiving God's forgiveness. Can anything be worth that price? Why do we hold on to what Jesus has called us to release?

For many, refusing to forgive is a weapon, the only

form of punishment we think the offender will ever receive. But in truth, the weapon of unforgiveness points a sword at our own soul.

For some, we keep rehearsing our wounds in the hope of discovering some insight that will finally make sense of all the pain. But in truth, every time we emotionally invest in reliving the hurt, we delay or even sabotage our own healing.

Jesus knows what it is like to be sinned against. He was slandered, betrayed, abused, mocked, misrepresented, beaten, and rejected. Yet He stayed on the cross and paid the price to offer forgiveness even to those would never admit their guilt or whisper, "I'm sorry."

The only way to abandon *rehash of the past* is to join Jesus on that cross and echo the words that set our souls free: *"Father, forgive them, for they do not know what they are doing."* (Luke 23:34)

☼ *Rehashing the past is spiritual poison.*

☼ *Refusing to forgive hinders us from receiving God's forgiveness.*

☼ *Jesus calls us to throw out the moldy leftovers of other's sins against us.*

MUCH OR LITTLE?

Then Jesus said to her, "Your sins are forgiven."

—LUKE 7:48

The guests reclined to enjoy the evening meal. Seated prominently at the table was Jesus' host, Simon, a respected Pharisee. On the dusty floor at Jesus' feet knelt a woman who had the reputation of being a sinner. When she heard that Jesus was near,

> She brought an alabaster jar of perfume, and as
> she stood behind him at his feet weeping, she
> began to wet his feet with her tears. Then she
> wiped them with her hair, kissed them and
> poured perfume on them. (Luke 7:37–38)

As we study this passage, let us prayerful reflect on whom we most identify with in this dinner of contrasts, Simon or the Sinner?

She was a religious outcast. He was a religious leader. Luke describes the woman as having lived a *sinful life*. This Greek word, *hamartōlos*, speaks of wickedness and devotion to sin. Simon, on the other hand, was a respected spiritual leader in his community; he was devoted to observing the Law.

She came to give. He came to judge. The woman brought her most precious treasure to give to the Savior. But many of the Pharisees were still undecided about Jesus. Simon had probably invited Jesus to dinner to observe Him more closely. Weighing this interaction with the woman, Simon's opinion of Jesus began to grow dim:

> *When the Pharisee who had invited him saw this, he said to himself, "If this man were a prophet, he would know who is touching him and what kind of woman she is—that she is a sinner."* (Luke 7:39)

She knew she was broken. He thought himself whole. The woman's sins were well-known. But her need to touch Jesus was greater than her fear of man's mocking. Risking public scorn, she wept, openly displaying her repentant heart. But her humility does not seem to inspire Simon to search his own soul. Apparently confident in his spiritual condition, Simon overestimates himself and, in doing so, underestimates Jesus.

He overlooked small gestures of service. She was grateful for the opportunity to serve.

Many Eastern cultures are known for their hospitality. Historians tell us that in New Testament times it would have been appropriate at a dinner such as this for the host to offer his guests water to wash their feet, oil for their dry skin, and an affectionate greeting. But for some unknown reason, Simon overlooked these common courtesies:

> Then he turned toward the woman and said to Simon, "Do you see this woman? I came into your house. You did not give me any water for my feet, but she wet my feet with her tears and wiped them with her hair. You did not give me a kiss, but this woman, from the time I entered, has not stopped kissing my feet. You did not put oil on my head, but she has poured perfume on my feet. Therefore, I tell you, her many sins have been forgiven—for she loved much. But he who has been forgiven little loves little." (Luke 7:44–47)

She loved much. He loved little. As the woman kissed, perfumed, and washed the Savior's feet, Jesus saw her love and Simon only saw her sin. Perhaps he did not know what true love looked like. But Jesus' eyes burn through reputations and appearances. Regardless of packaging, He draws near repentant souls. Simon had invited Jesus to a dinner. But the woman was inviting Jesus into her life:

> *Then Jesus said to her, "Your sins are forgiven."*
> *The other guests began to say among themselves,*
> *"Who is this who even forgives sins?" Jesus said to*
> *the woman, "Your faith has saved you; go in*
> *peace." (Luke 7:48–50)*

The sinner left forgiven. And Simon? As far as we know, he remained offended. Simon could not comprehend how a holy man would accept the touch of a sinful woman. Jesus could sit at his table, but he would not sit at Jesus' feet.

So what about us? Whom do we most resemble? Penitent sinners at the feet of the Savior or applauded leaders well-fed but spiritually dead at the head of the table?

Have we come to give or to judge? Do we know that we are broken or do we think ourselves whole? Have we let fear of man hinder us from discovering and expressing lavish affection for God?

May Jesus find in us humble hearts that love much!

☼ *Regardless of the "packaging," Jesus draws near to penitent souls.*

☼ *His forgiveness is lavish for those who weep at His feet.*

☼ *Those who know great forgiveness have great cause to love!*

THE SAFETY OF "SEARCH ME"

*Search me, O God, and know my heart; test me and know
my anxious thoughts. See if there is any offensive way in
me, and lead me in the way everlasting.*

—PSALM 139:23–24

When a crime is committed, we search the scene.
When disease devastates, we search for a cure.
When disaster strikes, we search for probable cause.

Most often, we call for a search *after* trouble arises.
But in Psalm 139, we find King David calling for a search
before a problem emerges. David's prayer in Psalm 51 was
a definite response to spiritual failure. However, Psalm
139:23–24 records not a desperate plea for post-failure
forgiveness but an earnest request for pre-problem
purification.

David begins this closing preventative prayer in Psalm
139 with two simple words: *search me.*

"Search me, O God." Webster defines *search* as "to
look into or over carefully or thoroughly in an effort to
find or discover something: to look through or explore by

inspecting possible places of concealment or investigating suspicious circumstances."

The Hebrew word for *search* in this passage is elsewhere translated *explore, inquire,* and *probe.* David's opening words of *"Search me, O God"* challenge us to volunteer as subjects of God's thorough and diligent examination.

"Know my heart." This same *know* in the Hebrew is used to describe God's intense friendship with Moses (*"No prophet has risen in Israel like Moses, whom the Lord knew face to face."* Deut. 34:10) and Adam's intimacy with Eve (*"And Adam knew Eve his wife."* Gen. 4:1 KJV). *Know* reflects the most intimate relationship possible between God and mankind.

David invites God to personally and completely be familiar with his *heart*—his entire being. No rooms are locked in this search. Nothing is marked "restricted access." *"Know my heart"* grants God full clearance to penetrate every shadowy corner of our very selves.

"Test me." With these words David asks God to inspect him for breaches of inner integrity. He longs for his faith to be utterly sincere because from personal experience David knew that his future could be sabotaged by unseen compromises. *"Test me"* is a request for God to examine the fabric of our lives for potentially fatal flaws.

"Know my anxious thoughts." Two English words (*anxious* + *thoughts*) are used to translate the Hebrew in this phrase. Together they paint a picture of a restless mind influenced by the whispers of fear. Our thought-life is often the venue of an ongoing, unseen wrestling match with worry. *"Know my anxious thoughts"* invites God to be our heart's coach and our mind's mentor.

"See if there is any offensive way in me." Here we find a wonderful twist. David is not only concerned about issues that could hurt him, He is concerned about anything that could hurt or offend God! The New Living Bible translates this phrase, *"Point out anything in me that offends you."* These words move us past man's expectations, religious codes of conduct, known laws, and Biblical commandments into the inner room of a love that yearns to fulfill not just God's requirements but God's personal desires. *"See if there is any offensive way in me"* reflects a longing to live in such a way that we never grieve the heart of God.

"Lead me in the way everlasting." Proverbs 14:12 states, *"There is a way that seems right to a man, but in the end it leads to death."* David's predecessor, Saul, exemplified a leader who took the "way" of man. David desperately did not want to go down Saul's path. *"Lead me in*

the way everlasting" asks God to guide us into His (not man's) ways.

What safety there is in standing before our merciful God and echoing David's simple prayer! How assuring it is to be fully known—and fully loved! Every morning, *search me* grants us the opportunity to sit in on God's briefing regarding the state of our hearts. As He warns or convicts, His love leads us in repentance. We rise from prayer with a clear conscience and a sound confidence that God will continue to guide us into all truth and ultimately into His eternal arms.

☼ *Wisdom invites God to search us even before a problem arises.*

☼ *To be effective, the invitation must grant God unrestricted access to our hearts.*

☼ *Prayed sincerely, "Search me," keeps us safely on God's good path.*

DUSTY ALTARS

*I know your deeds, your hard work and your perseverance
. . . yet . . . you have forsaken your first love.*
—REVELATION 2:2, 4

The sun streamed through the stained glass window and revealed a thick film of dust on the old church's altars. Untouched, the coating looked like soft gray snow. Dust on the altar? How could we not notice?

Perhaps we have just been busy (working for the Lord of course.) Perhaps we do not need or use the altars as much now (after all our seats are padded.) Perhaps we noticed the dust but have been waiting for someone else to do something about it (our gifts are best used elsewhere). Or perhaps somewhere along the way we simply stopped caring.

Whatever the reason, there the dust lies . . . on those old wooden altars once watered with tears . . . and on the altars of our hearts, neglected for years.

Like us, the church in Ephesus was too busy to notice the dust collecting around their hearts. In the book of

Revelation, God affirms them for their hard work, their patient endurance, their refusal to tolerate wickedness, and their testing of false apostles. These good folks demonstrated good deeds, pure doctrine, and proven perseverance.

But it simply was not enough. God longed for something *more*. He longed for something they had before: *"You have forsaken your first love."* (Rev. 2:4) The Greek word here translated *forsaken* is also used by Paul in 1 Corinthians 7:11 but there it is translated *divorce*. *Forsaken* means *to dismiss, to send away*, and *to leave behind*.

This hard-working church in Ephesus left God behind. In the midst of serving, they forgot to love. Somehow, knowledge and activity had stepped in as substitutes for intimacy.

What do we do when we see a coating of dust on the altar of our heart? What do we do when we realize that we too have forsaken our first Love? In Revelation 2:5, Jesus offers us this counsel: *remember, repent, and rewind.*

"Remember the height from which you have fallen!" First, Jesus calls us to *remember* how much we used to love God. This can be a heartbreaking exercise because it requires us to acknowledge broken promises and postponed commitments: "I will spend more time with God

116

after . . ." However painful, we must hold the memory of how much we used to love God tightly and let it stand in stark contrast with our lukewarm love today.

"Repent." Next, Jesus counsels us to *repent*, to change our minds about our sin and consequently change our lives. Love has no understudies, stunt doubles, or pinch hitters. Nothing can take its place.

"Do the things you did at first." Finally, Jesus encourages us to *rewind*. What did we used to do when we loved God more than life itself? For some it may be singing, for others reading. For a few it may be journaling or taking long walks in the park. For others it will be intercession or sharing their faith, small groups, or Bible study. Whatever is was, however simplistic it may now seem, we need to "do the thing" we "did at first."

Remember, repent, rewind . . . and realize a fresh, new, dust-free love for your Savior.

☼ *Knowledge and activity offer themselves as substitutes for intimacy with God.*

☼ *God longs to be our First Love.*

☼ *In the midst of serving, we must not forget to love.*

RESTING IN
GOD'S WORD

AS GOOD AS HIS WORD

My word that goes out from my mouth: It will not return to me empty.

—ISAIAH 55:11

Generations ago, our elders were taught that, "a man is only as good as his word." The adage represented a belief that you could judge someone's character by his ability to make and keep promises.

But beliefs in general, and promises in particular, are more questioned than trusted in our day. An epidemic of broken promises has left us wondering if anyone's word is reliable. So when others make promises, we smile politely and wisely ask them to sign this legal document, that official contract, or those binding agreements so that we are protected in the event they fail to keep their word.

But there is One who has never failed to keep His word. There is One whose words have never been empty and whose promises have never been broken. This One has vowed that His Word will never return void:

> *As the rain and the snow come down from heaven, and do not return to it without watering the earth and making it bud and flourish, so that it yields seed for the sower and bread for the eater, so is my word that goes out from my mouth: It will not return to me empty, but will accomplish what I desire and achieve the purpose for which I sent it.* (Isa. 55:10–11)

The law of gravity promises that, once released from the clouds, rain will fall. And once released from His mouth, God's character promises that His Word will never fail. It certainly never failed when it was released from Jesus' mouth.

The apostle John stated that, *"The Word became flesh and made his dwelling among us. We have seen his glory, the glory of the One and Only, who came from the Father."* (John 1:14) Through a mystery we can only faintly comprehend, God's spoken Word walked among us in the Person of Jesus Christ. And wherever His words fell, life grew.

Jesus said, *"Be clean!"* and a leper was cured. (Matt. 8:3)

Jesus said, *"Take your mat and go home"* and a paralytic walked out the door. (Matt. 9:6)

Jesus said, *"Stretch out your hand"* and a man's shriveled arm was restored. (Matt. 12:13)

Jesus said, *"Your request is granted"* and a mother's daughter was healed. (Matt. 15:28)

Jesus said *"Come out of him!"* and an oppressed man knew peace. (Mark 1:25)

Jesus said, *"Be freed"* and a sick woman stopped bleeding. (Mark 5:34)

Jesus said, *"Be opened"* and a man could hear and speak. (Mark 7:34)

Jesus said, *"Go, your faith has healed you"* and Bartimaeus received his sight. (Mark 10:52)

Jesus said, *"Get up"* to a widow's dead son and a funeral turned into a dance. (Luke 7:14)

Jesus said, *"Your sins are forgiven"* and a prostitute felt peace. (Luke 7:48)

Jesus said, *"My child, get up!"* and a father's grief turned to tears of joy. (Luke 8:54)

Jesus said, *"You are set free"* and a crippled woman stood tall. (Luke 13:12)

Jesus said, *"I who speak to you am he"* and a Samaritan woman believed. (John 4:26)

Jesus said, *"Neither do I condemn you"* and an adulteress received a second chance. (John 8:11)

Jesus said, *"Come out!"* and Lazarus emerged from his tomb. (John 11:43)

Jesus said, *"It is finished"* and the barrier separating us from God was torn in two. (John 19:30)

God has not stopped speaking. The Bible is filled with His Words. None of them are empty. None of them will fail. His Word can still make us whole. His Word still brings peace to the troubled and hope to the grieving. His Word still cleanses hearts and brings life to the dead. His Word still IS. And our God *is* as good as His Word!

☼ *God's words have never been empty.*

☼ *His spoken Word walked among us in fullness through Jesus.*

☼ *Wherever Jesus' wonderful words fall, life grows!*

CHARTING A NEW COURSE

He did what was right in the sight of the LORD.

—2 KINGS 22:2

Are we doomed to make the same mistakes the generations before us have made? If our families were filled with rage, will our tempers one day become uncontrollable? If our parents were unfaithful, are we destined for failed marriages? If our relatives had addictions, is it just a matter of time until we do?

In a word, NO!

Certainly we are greatly influenced by our environment and our genes. But the choices (good or bad) of previous generations cannot write our history. Their past does not dictate our future, because—more than nurture or nature—our futures are forged by our *wills*. What will we do with what we have inherited? When we align our wills with God and His Word, we can chart a new course for our lives.

Consider the example of Josiah.

Josiah's grandfather, Manasseh, was a wicked man.

During his fifty-five year reign as King of Judah, he led the people into idolatry and horrible sin. He set up altars to worship demons in God's temple and practiced sorcery and child sacrifice. Scripture records that Manasseh, *"did much evil in the sight of the LORD, provoking him to anger."* (2 Kings 21:6)

Josiah's dad, Amon, followed in his father's footsteps. He became King of Judah at the age of twenty-two. In his brief two year reign, *"he did evil in the sight of the LORD, as his father Manasseh had done. . . . He forsook the LORD, the God of his fathers, and did not walk in the way of the LORD."* (2 Kings 21:20, 22)

Amon's own officials assassinated him. They in turn were killed by the people of the land who then placed eight-year-old Josiah on the chaos-filled throne of his father.

What a beginning! In addition to inheriting a blood-stained crown, Josiah had a spiritual heritage that no one would want. All he saw as a boy growing up in the palace was idolatry, witchcraft, immorality, and injustice. And his dad was one of the chief sinners of the country!

Surely, if anyone could have been doomed to make the mistakes of previous generations it would have been Josiah. But Josiah's life clearly demonstrates that God gives each soul the power to choose His ways.

At the age of sixteen, Josiah *"began to seek the God of his father David."* (2 Chron. 34:3) Four years later he started leading his people slowly into spiritual reform. Not only did Josiah choose not to walk in the ways of his father and grandfather, Josiah chose to guide his nation back to God.

When he was twenty-six, Josiah made a discovery that became the guiding force for the rest of his life. This treasure made the difference between him being a young man who started well and a grown man who finished well! Josiah discovered the Word of God.

> *Hilkiah the priest found the Book of the Law of the LORD given by Moses. . . . Shapan* [the scribe] *read it before the king. Thus it happened, when the king heard the words of the Law, that he tore his clothes.* (2 Chron. 34:14, 18–19, NKJV)

Josiah was deeply distressed when he heard about the judgments his kingdom had brought on itself through disobedience. In his heart, he had always wanted to do the right thing; now God's Word showed him how to do the right thing. The rest of his life was spent purging the land of idolatry and impurity and reintroducing the people of Judah to their God.

So let us return to our opening question: Are we doomed to make the same mistakes the generations before us have made?

Absolutely not! As we, like Josiah, align ourselves with God and His Word, we will find the strength to chart a new course for our lives.

☼ *We are not destined to repeat the sins of previous generations.*

☼ *More than by nurture or nature, our futures are forged by our wills.*

☼ *Empowered by God's Word, we can choose to leave a legacy of godliness for the next generation.*

IT IS WRITTEN

Man does not live on bread alone, but on every word that comes from the mouth of God.

—MATTHEW 4:4

The tension is too familiar: we *know* what the right choice is, but something deep within is hungry for the *feeling* the wrong choice produces.

We know we should not gossip, but it makes us feel valuable when others see us as a source of important information. We know we should give to the needy, but it feels so good to spend that money pampering ourselves. We know those friends are a poor influence on us, but they make us feel so special when we are with them. We know we struggle with discontentment or jealousy or greed or fear or impurity every time we watch this or read that, but it feels so relaxing to totally escape.

"Resist the devil, and he will flee from you," Scripture counsels. (James 4:7) But how do we find the strength to overcome the feeling and choose what we know is right?

Jesus understood this tension. He faced it in extreme

128

measures during His ministry on earth. How did He resist the devil? How did He position *feel good* behind *is good*?

Immediately after being baptized by John in the Jordan, the Holy Spirit guided Jesus into the desert where Jesus experienced intense temptation and testing in preparation for the challenging years ahead.

Three times the devil came to Jesus and tempted Him to disobey Father God. Three times, Jesus resisted the devil and the devil fled. Let us examine how Jesus fought temptation and won.

> *After fasting forty days and forty nights, he was hungry. The tempter came to him and said, "If you are the Son of God, tell these stones to become bread."* (Matt. 4:2–3)

God led Jesus into a supernatural fast. Jesus was hungry (understandably) but knew He needed to look to His Father (and not His own power) for provision. Satan challenged Jesus to turn stones into food and satisfy His hunger. Note how Jesus responds to this first temptation:

> *"It is written: 'Man does not live on bread alone but on every word that comes from the mouth of God.'"* (Matt. 4:4)

Jesus did not resist the devil by asking His emotions for their opinion. He fought temptation not with *"I feel"* but with *"It is written!"* Jesus remembered, recited, and stood upon God's Word.

Since the Word of God is actual power for living, it strengthened Jesus to resist temptation not just once but over and over again:

> *Then the devil took him to the holy city and had him stand on the highest point of the temple. "If you are the Son of God," he said, "throw yourself down.". . . Jesus answered him, "It is also written: 'Do not put the Lord your God to the test.'"* (Matt. 4:5–7)
>
> *Again, the devil took him to a very high mountain and showed him all the kingdoms of the world and their splendor. "All this I will give you," he said, "if you will bow down and worship me." Jesus said to him, "Away from me Satan! For it is written: 'Worship the Lord your God, and serve him only.'"* (Matt. 4:8–10)

In the battle between *feel good* and *is good*, Jesus relied on God's Word for victory. That same powerful Word is still available to us today.

"Easy for Jesus, hard for us," we may sigh as we stare at our Bible feeling overwhelmed at its depth and breadth. But we must remember that Jesus drew strength to resist temptation from three verses of the Bible, not three hundred. In fact, all of the Scripture He called upon came from within a five-chapter section of one book of the Bible, Deuteronomy.

We do not have to have a Ph.D. or photographic memory to call upon God's Word. We simply need to get the Scriptures inside of us. As we store God's Word in our hearts, we will find ourselves strengthened in the place of temptation to choose what *is* right instead of what feels right.

☼ *Temptation is the voice that entices us to position "feels good" in front of "is good."*

☼ *Jesus resisted temptation by calling upon God's Word.*

☼ *The Scriptures do more than inspire us, they equip us to live for God.*

JOY ALONE

A farmer went out to sow his seed . . . .

—MATTHEW 13:3

Matthew, Mark, and Luke all record the Parable of the Sower. Jesus shared this story with a large group who had gathered to hear Him teach by the lake. The parable tells the tale of a farmer who scattered seed that fell on four different types of ground, the second of which is our present focus.

Some of the farmer's seeds fell on the path only to be eaten by the birds. Other seed,

> *fell on rocky places, where it did not have much soil. It sprang up quickly, because the soil was shallow. But when the sun came up, the plants were scorched, and they withered because they had no root.* (Matt. 13:5–6)

Some of the seed fell among thorns that grew and choked the plants. Still other seed fell on good soil and produced a harvest.

After the crowds left, the disciples came to Jesus privately and asked Him about the parable. Of the second type of ground Jesus explained that,

> *The one who received the seed that fell on rocky places is the man who heard the word and at once receives it with joy. But since he has no root, he lasts only a short time. When trouble or persecution comes because of the word, he quickly falls away.* (Matt. 13:20–21)

The seed that fell on rocky places represents those who at first receive God's Word with joy. They are excited, exuberant . . . and in danger.

These happy hearts are at risk because they have no roots. They may *spring up quickly,* but their outward growth is not an indication of inward strength. Under the surface, they are extremely vulnerable.

Those represented by the second seed are joy-full but root-less. Jesus explains that though these seeds may live for a little while, in the time of testing they stumble and fall away. (See also Luke 8:13.)

Evidently, receiving the Word with joy is simply not enough. Which makes sense, because joy is a fruit of our faith, not a root of our faith—and plants simply do not grow fruit down, they grow root up.

Though highly sought after, joy alone has little holding power. Happiness is easily intimidated in a time of testing. To survive, our faith needs to be anchored in something much more substantial than pleasant emotions. According to Jesus' parable, those who flourish not only happily hear the Word, they faithfully obey the Word: *"The seed on good soil stands for those with a noble and good heart, who hear the word, retain it, and by persevering produce a crop."* (Luke 8:15)

Sounds like work! Enduring faith is anchored in tenacious perseverance in God's Word.

Of this happy but rootless second type of ground, Luke adds that, *"the plants withered because they had no moisture."* (Luke 8.6) In times of drought, only trees with deep root systems survive. If our roots are in obedience to God's Word, our souls will continue to be moist even when our circumstances are dry.

So when the heat of trouble or persecution causes our faith to feel faint, we would be wise to examine our root structure. Perhaps we have spent more time pursuing joy than rooting God's Word deep in our hearts. Without the anchor of tenacious perseverance in God's

Word, Jesus tells us that even the joyful will *"wither"* and *"fall away."*

Hot days are ahead. Therefore, let us not place our hope in *springing up quickly* or the fruit of *joy*, but let us anchor our faith in the ever-expanding, drought-proof roots of obedience to God's Word.

- ☼ *Joy is a fruit—not a root—of our faith. Alone it is insufficient to make faith flourish.*

- ☼ *Enduring faith is rooted in tenacious obedience to God's Word.*

- ☼ *The deep roots of God's Word will water our faith in the scorching heat of adversity.*

RELISH THE RICHES

Humbly accept the word planted in you, which can save you.

—JAMES 1:21

How do we rest in God's Word? As the Bible sits in our hands, how do we actually get its truth into our hearts? In the book that bears his name, James offers three principles that can help us make God's Word our restful refuge.

Humbly accept the word planted in you, which can save you. (James 1:21) The Greek word translated *humbly* (*prautēs*) more often appears as *gentle* or *gentleness*. This same *gentleness* is listed in Galatians 5:23 as one of the fruits of the Spirit. We are to approach God's Word meekly, in humility, with the posture of a receptive learner. And we are to actively welcome the implanting, engrafting, and establishment of God's Word in us. The image of planting that James uses was especially appropriate for the agrarian society of his original audience. The image communicates intentionality, process, and the expectation of growth.

So as we open God's Word, let us come with hungry,

teachable hearts, confident that fruitfulness awaits us. Think of each verse as a life-giving seed. As we read, listen, and study, these saving seeds are planted in our spirits and truth begins to grow from within!

Do not merely listen to the word, and so deceive yourselves. Do what it says. (James 1:22) One of the great themes in the book of James is that, *"faith without deeds is dead."* (James 2:26) When it comes to the Scriptures, listening without doing breeds deception.

Each day as we conclude our time in God's Word, we must ask, "What does this mean for me now?" Every passage of the Bible offers a principle to apply, a warning to heed, or an example to follow.

"Even all those *begats* and *cubits*?" one might ask. Oh yes! Many of the names recorded in biblical lineages represent fascinating stories. The genealogies themselves can inspire us to be thankful for our heritage, to visit an elderly saint, or spend time investing in the next generation. In addition to their rich symbolism, all the *cubits* and extensive explanations of preparations for the tabernacle and the temple can encourage appreciation for God's attention to detail in our lives or call us to pay attention to the unseen.

Nothing in the Bible is ornamental. All of God's Words offer timeless instruction for our lives.

Look intently into the perfect law that gives freedom, and continue to do this, not forgetting what you have heard. (from James 1:25) What do we do after we have read the Scriptures with humility, intentionally planted God's Word in our hearts, and—to the best of our ability— acted on what we have learned? According to James, we continue doing more of the same!

Look intently, which is translated from the Greek *parakyptō*, means *to bend over to observe* or *to stoop over to see*. As an eager scientist approaches the lab or an expectant archeologist approaches the dig, James calls us to keep approaching God's Word enthusiastically. The treasures of the Bible are inexhaustible!

Since God's Word is living, it is ever-fresh and new. Even if we were to read the entire Bible through a hundred times, its pages would never grow stale. As we faithfully and actively study the Scriptures, we will find ourselves resting in and relishing the riches of God's Word.

☼ *Every book in the Bible has relevance for our lives today.*

☼ *The Scriptures plant life-giving seeds of truth in our spirit.*

☼ *Riches of wisdom await all who approach God's Word with hungry, humble hearts.*

THE KING AND THE SCROLL

When he takes the throne of his kingdom, he is to write for himself on a scroll a copy of this law.

—DEUTERONOMY 17:18

The fifth book of the Bible takes its name from instructions Moses gave regarding kings: *"He is to write for himself on a scroll a copy of this law."* *Copy of this law* was rendered "second law" or "repetition of the law," hence the name Deuteronomy.

For ease in reference, Deuteronomy has been organized into 34 chapters. Moses' directions regarding kings are found in the middle of the book in chapter 17.

First, Moses advises the people to appoint only a king that God has chosen from among their own people. Next, he establishes four rules for the king (vv. 16–18):

1. Do not return to Egypt to get more horses because God said not to *"go back that way again."*

2. Do not take many wives or your *"heart will be led astray."*

3. Do not store up a lot of treasure.

And from our key verse:

4. When you become king, handwrite on a scroll a copy of these laws.

Kings were surrounded by servants who did everything from making their food to manicuring their feet. But the text seems to imply that Moses required a king to do one thing solo: *"write for himself"* a copy of the law. In Hebrew, the word translated *law* is *Torah,* which refers not just to Moses' address but to the entire Pentateuch, the Bible's first five books.

This may have accounted for the first royal case of writer's cramp. Mr. King was to hand-copy not merely 34 chapters and 959 verses from Deuteronomy, but 187 chapters and 5858 verses of the entire Torah!

Speed writing in English, we might clock in at one verse a minute, so—for the sake of discussion—let us grant royal, kingly writing in Hebrew ninety seconds a verse. If the king devoted an hour every day to handwriting a copy of the Law, he could spend the first 146 days of his reign completing the task.

Do you know what that would do? Keep him out of trouble! Because day after day he would read, write, and live the story of God's creation and man's fall, Israel's rebellion and God's deliverance, the ten commandments and the blessings of obedience. And, since it is close to impossible to multi-task when copying something by hand, the king would daily spend time focused exclusively upon engaging God through the Scriptures.

Once completed, Moses tells the king to keep this copy with him at all times and *"read it all the days of his life."* (v.19) So in summary: Write out God's Words, keep them near always, and call upon them daily.

Why? Moses answers this question for us:

> *So that he may learn to revere the LORD his God and follow carefully all the words of this law and these decrees and not consider himself better than his brothers and turn from the law to the right or to the left. Then he and his descendants will reign a long time over this kingdom in Israel.*
> (Deut. 17:19–20)

Whether one is a king or a child of the King, internalizing God's Word guarantees certain eternally weighty results:

We develop a holy reverence for and fear of God. (Helpful, because kings are not the only ones who quickly forget Who is actually on the throne.)

We walk in humility toward the rest of humanity.
(Imagine what that could produce in our homes, work-places, and communities!)

God's Word becomes an internal map to keep us on the path of obedience. (Great news for anyone who knows what it is like to truly be lost.)

Our children inherit a blessing of God's favor. (Whatever it means, sign us up!)

Feel much or feel little, see stars or fight sleep . . . if we daily engage God's Word these fruits *will* emerge in our lives.

The Bible, thankfully, is more than great literature and interesting history. God's Word is alive and filled with real power! It changes hearts, renews minds, and—if heeded—guides us to the safety of Heaven.

☼ *Daily interaction with God's Word keeps us out of unnecessary trouble.*

☼ *Write out God's Words, keep them near always, and call upon them daily!*

☼ *Internalizing God's Word blesses us, those we are near, and the generations to come.*

SWEET CONSEQUENCES

The ordinances of the LORD are sure and altogether right-eous. They are more precious than gold, than much pure gold; they are sweeter than honey, than honey from the comb. By them is your servant warned; in keeping them there is great reward.

—PSALM 19:9–11

*C*onsequence.

What a solemn word! Generally it brings to mind the unwanted (and somewhat embarrassing) results of less than wise decisions . . . like continuing to drive when that little red light begins to flash . . . or throwing pants in the wash without checking their pockets . . . or forgetting that special birthday . . . or asking that slightly plump new acquaintance when her baby is due. But by definition, consequences are not always negative; they simply refer to the fruit of a decision, action, or other cause.

King David teaches us about the consequences of keeping God's Word. He calls these consequences *great rewards*. *Great*, in the Hebrew, refers to *abundance*. The word *reward* refers to cause or consequence and is more often rendered *because*. In Psalm 19, David celebrates the abundantly sweet consequences of submitting to God's Word.

Do you need a new start?

> *The law of the LORD is perfect,*
> *reviving the soul.* (Ps. 19:7)

Perfection here implies completeness and soundness. The law (*Torah*) of God is complete—no pieces are missing. It is entirely sound—like a lake frozen solid, you can stand on it with confidence.

The Hebrew word translated *reviving* literally means *turning back* or *returning*. God's laws help return our souls to the safety of God Himself. The law of the Lord empowers a life to turn back to God!

Do you need practical wisdom for living?

> *The statutes of the LORD are trustworthy,*
> *making wise the simple.* (Ps. 19:7)

In our day of hollow promises and promotional overstatements, we desperately need a source of reliable advice.

God's statutes (regulations or laws) are truly *trustworthy*. They are confirmed, supported, and worthy of belief.

God's rules are relevant; they hold up in real life. They give *wisdom* (prudence; practical understanding) to *simple* people. The Hebrew word here translated *simple* refers to being naïve, easily swayed or manipulated.

The laws of God are a safeguard for those of us who are just a wee bit naïve. They provide practical counsel even for impractical people! What great news: God's Word is a trustworthy source of wisdom for daily life.

Do you need reliable direction?

> *The precepts of the LORD are right,*
> *giving joy to the heart.* (Ps. 19:8)

All of us know spatially-disoriented people whom we would NEVER ask for directions unless we had a few extra hours (or days) to spend hopelessly lost.

In Psalm 19:8, the word *precepts* refers to directional instruction. David assures us that God's directions are *right*: they are straight, not crooked. These reliable directions bring gladness to the entire person—the inner soul, the heart.

Imagine that we were at sea on a ship without a

compass. In peaceful weather we might be able to convince ourselves that all was well, but a storm would reveal the true danger we were in. God's Word is the always-accurate, never-failing compass of our souls! Even in the midst of the fiercest storm, His directions are entirely reliable.

Do you need light for your soul?

> *The commands of the LORD are radiant,*
> *giving light to the eyes.* (Ps.19:8)

The term *radiant* carries a sense of moral purity and enlightenment. God's commands are so utterly pure and uncontaminated that they shine. Their radiance brings light to our eyes.

In the Hebrew language, the word for *eyes* was used to describe more than the physical organ of sight. Genesis 3:7 records that after Adam and Eve ate the forbidden fruit, *"the eyes of both of them were opened."* In Jeremiah 5:21, the prophet calls out to, *"foolish and senseless people, who have eyes but do not see."* The *eye* represents our ability to perceive; our moral and spiritual understanding.

God's commands give light to our *eyes* so that in a world filled with darkness we can see and perceive Truth.

A new start, wisdom for living, reliable direction, light for the soul . . . these are just a few of the many sweet consequences that are ours when we treasure God's Word!

☼ *God's Word is solid. We can stand upon it with confidence.*

☼ *God's laws are relevant. They provide practical wisdom for daily life.*

☼ *God's Word is our trustworthy navigator, lighting our path with truth.*

RESTING IN
GOD'S COMFORT

WHEN DREAMS DIE

Unless a kernel of wheat falls to the ground and dies, it remains only a single seed. But if it dies, it produces many seeds.

—JOHN 12:24

Buried any dreams lately?

We thought our dreams were God's dreams. We prayed, believed, made plans and worked hard. But now it is over.

So here we sit, graveside, by our lifeless hopes. And as we sit, we begin to doubt. "Did I miss something? Should I have prayed or done more? Or perhaps I never really heard God in the first place. If *this* was not God's will, then how can I trust myself to ever think I hear Him?!"

Jesus' disciples knew exactly how we feel. They too had a dream that was cruelly crucified before their very eyes. They were certain their dream was God's dream but then their hoped-for Messiah was murdered. Not even a fool could hope after that. The sealed tomb confirmed the truth: Jesus was dead.

Today we speed read through the darkest days of the disciple's lives because we know that the joy of the resurrection is only a few verses away. But if we slow down there is much to learn. What did they do after their dream died on the cross? How did they cope? Let us walk with the disciples as they mourned the death of the greatest dream they had ever known:

> *All His acquaintances . . . stood at a distance, watching these things. . . . [Joseph] went to Pilate and asked for the body of Jesus. Then he took it down, wrapped it in linen, and placed it in a tomb.* (Luke 23:49, 52–53, NKJV)

Speechless, Jesus' followers kept watch until the very end. They held on to flickering hope until its flame was extinguished. Then they gave themselves permission to bury their dream. Burial is a symbol of respect.

When dreams shatter, we too need to give ourselves time to gently collect the broken pieces and wrap them respectfully in tears. This is not about prematurely abandoning hope. This is about accepting reality. Denying Jesus' death would not return Him to the disciples. It was healthy for them to permit a burial. Faith is not threatened by funerals.

And the women . . . observed the tomb and how
His body was laid. Then they returned and pre-
pared spices and fragrant oils. And they rested on
the Sabbath according to the commandment.
(Luke 23:55–56, NKJV)

Jesus' followers lingered by His tomb, then they returned home to prepare spices and oils to preserve and honor Him in His death.

Those who have lost loved-ones may need to linger in that favorite old chair. The entrepreneur may need unhurried days (instead of one angry hour) to reminisce as she packs up an office after an unsuccessful business venture. In response to that rejection letter, the student may need to head for the mountains to refresh his faith. Or the one who suffered a miscarriage may need to give herself permission to mourn instead of rushing to put everything away.

Take the time. Prepare the spices. Preserve and honor the memories. Rest. The women rested after Jesus' death. Rest is essential—a need, not a luxury—if we are to remain healthy through the burial of dreams.

Two of them were going to a village called
Emmaus. . . . They were talking with each other

152

about everything that had happened. (Luke
24:13–14)

Like the followers of Jesus, when dreams die we need
to enjoy good talks and take long walks with trusted
friends. The disciples did not isolate themselves after
Jesus' burial. They intentionally maintained their relationships. We, too, must resist isolation. Even in loss—
especially in loss—we are stronger together than alone.

> *As they talked and discussed these things with*
> *each other, Jesus himself came up and walked*
> *along with them; but they were kept from recog-*
> *nizing him.* (Luke 24:15–16)

The disciples did not know it, but as they walked
with each other, Jesus walked with them. They could not
comprehend it, but their dream, though dead, had not
perished!

Most of us will not see the resurrection of our
dreams within three days. In fact, some of our dreams are
sown for future generations to reap. Even then, obedience is never a waste; it is an investment in a future we
cannot see. When we dream with God, even in burial,

our dreams are not lost, they are planted. God never forgets the *"kernel of wheat that falls to the ground and dies."* (John 12:24)

What grows from that painful planting is God's business. But sowing in faith is ours, and our faithfulness is never sown in vain.

☼ *When dreams die, take time to rest, remember, and walk with others.*

☼ *Obedience is an investment in a future we cannot see.*

☼ *God never forgets our buried dreams.*

COME HOME

We had to celebrate and be glad, because this brother of yours was dead and is alive again; he was lost and is found!

—LUKE 15:32

Sometimes it is hard to go back home, especially when "home" is God and we have been away for many years. Uncertain, we wrestle in our minds with reasons why it is too late to return to Him.

- If I had more to offer Him, maybe. But I can't ask God to take me in now.

- I'm too ashamed to return home. I've ruined everything He ever gave me.

- No, thank you. God is probably mad at me, and I don't blame Him.

- I've tried, but I just don't have what it takes to serve God.

- I would only disappoint Him again.

- After all this time? It would be wrong to offer God the little that's left of my life.

- I don't deserve forgiveness. I'll never forgive myself.

- Does God truly want me anymore?

- I'm really not worth saving.

In Luke 15, Jesus tells the story of a man who also struggled with these thoughts as he considered returning to his father. He had left home as a young man full of cash and confidence but ran out of both simultaneously:

> "The younger one said to his father, 'Father, give me my share of the estate.' So he divided his property between them. Not long after that, the younger son got together all he had, set off for a distant country and there squandered his wealth in wild living.
>
> After he had spent everything, there was a severe famine in that whole country, and he began to be in need." (Luke 15:12–14)

In need is elsewhere translated *lack, inferior to, destitute,* and *fall short.* His pockets were empty and he felt like a failure, but he was either too embarrassed or too proud to return home. So he took a local job feeding pigs. The contrast between his father and this employer was drastic. The new boss did not give him anything to eat, while his dad's servants had food to spare. While the pigs grew fatter, he grew thinner and finally decided it was time to go home:

> "I will set out and go back to my father and say to him: 'Father, I have sinned against heaven and against you. I am no longer worthy to be called your son: make me like one of your hired men.'"
> (Luke 15:18–19)

If his steps were light at first, they probably grew heavier as he drew closer to home and doubt invited him to question his decision: *I left with much, I'm retuning with nothing. What will dad say? Surely he's upset with me. Is it even fair for me to ask him to take me back? What if I just disappoint him again? After all I've done, I don't deserve his forgiveness. I don't even deserve to be called his child!*

But at this point in the story, Jesus offers words of great comfort for all who, like this man, are thinking of returning home:

"But while he was still along way off, his father saw him and was filled with compassion for him; he ran to his son, threw his arms around him and kissed him. . . . The father said to his servants, 'Quick! Bring the best robe and put it on him. Put a ring on his finger and sandals on his feet. Bring the fattened calf and kill it. Let's have a feast and celebrate. For this son of mine was dead and is alive again; he was lost and is found.'" (Luke 15:20, 22–24)

The truth is that Father God never gives up hope for us. He never takes His eyes off of us. When we begin to turn back toward Him, compassion floods His heart and He runs toward us. Wrapping us in His arms He shouts, "My daughter has come home! My son has returned! Clothe them and feed them with the best from My house!"

"But I don't deserve such acceptance," we protest. True. But who among us does? God's acceptance is not based upon who we are or what we have done. God's acceptance is based on who He is, and what He has done. That is why we call Him Savior.

That Savior is still calling, "Come home, My child, come home!"

☼ *Father God is waiting for us to come home.*

☼ *When we turn toward God, His compassionate arms welcome us sincerely.*

☼ *None of us deserve such acceptance, but such is the gift of God.*

THE FEAR OF MAN

I, even I, am he who comforts you. Who are you that you
fear mortal men, the sons of men who are but grass, that
you forget the LORD your Maker?

—ISAIAH 51:12–13

The sting of other's anger.
The pain of disapproval.
The shame of being blamed.

We are not the first to fear the wounding words and ways of man:

> *"Hear me, you who know what is right, you peo-*
> *ple who have my law in your hearts: Do not fear*
> *the reproach of men or be terrified by their*
> *insults."* (Isa. 51:7)

Those who loved God in Isaiah's day lived with the realities of political and spiritual oppression. Here, and throughout the Scriptures, God gives His people of all generations two weapons to fight the fear of man in our hearts:

Remember who He is, and remember who they are.
He is God!

> *"I, even I, am he who comforts you . . . the* LORD
> *your Maker, who stretched out the heavens and
> laid the foundations of the earth.*
>
> *For I am the* LORD *your God, who churns up
> the seas so that its waves roar—the* LORD
> *Almighty is his name.*
>
> *I have put my words in your mouth and cov-
> ered you with the shadow of my hand—I who set
> the heavens in place, who laid the foundations of
> the earth, and who say to Zion, 'You are my peo-
> ple.'"* (Isa. 51:12–13, 15–16)

They are not!

> *"Who are you that you fear mortal men, the sons
> of men, who are but grass?*
>
> *For the moth will eat them up like a garment;
> the worm will devour them like wool. But my
> righteousness will last forever, my salvation
> through all generations."* (Isa. 51:12, 8)

SITTING IN GOD'S SUNSHINE

These images are rather severe, but so is the truth God is presenting before us.

God tells us that we do not have to live in fear of other's words or actions against us because they, like we, are destined to become dust. Regardless how loud their shouts or how abusive their ways, they too are mortal. We will all die. And after we die, we will all stand before God, and His righteousness endures forever!

Humanity is fragile, frail, and finite. But God is unshakeable, strong, and eternal. He is divine. He cannot die. And by grace (and grace alone) He calls us His people.

These two weapons have been used successfully to fight the fear of man by God's people for thousands of years.

King David, whose life was always in danger, wrote: *"When I am afraid, I will trust in you. In God whose word I praise, in God I trust; I will not be afraid. What can mortal man do to me?"* (Ps. 56:3–4)

Solomon, who also had enemies in his land and whisperers in his courts, wrote that the, *"fear of man will prove to be a snare, but whoever trusts in the LORD is kept safe."* (Prov. 29:25)

And Jesus commands His followers: *"Do not be afraid of those who kill the body but cannot kill the soul. Rather, be*

afraid of the One who can destroy both soul and body in hell."
(Matt. 10:28)

What can people actually do to us?

They can stain our reputations, but God fully knows all hearts. They can stand in the way of opportunity, but God opens doors that no man can close. They can steal our earthly goods, but God is our true treasure. They can restrict our physical freedom, but God's Spirit is unchained. They can hinder or take our jobs, but God is our Provider. They can even kill our body, but they cannot touch our souls.

So the next time we feel threatened by someone's words or ways, let us resist the fear of people by remembering these two truths:

1. The person that stands before us is human.
2. The One that stands behind us is God.

☼ *God's knows that we are vulnerable to the hurtful ways and words of others.*

☼ *God calls us to remember Him when we are tempted to fear man.*

☼ *Mankind is mortal, God is not, and He is the One we will stand before in the end.*

163

MORE THAN A
SENTIMENTAL CARD

*Praise be to the God and Father of our Lord Jesus Christ,
the Father of compassion and the God of all comfort, who
comforts us in all our troubles, so that we can comfort
those in any trouble with the comfort we ourselves have
received from God.*

—2 CORINTHIANS 1:3–4

Second Corinthians chapter one could be called the comfort chapter. Within four verses, comfort is mentioned eight times. As used by Paul, the Greek word translated *comfort* (*parakaléō*) refers to strengthening another through exhortation or encouragement.

Paul identifies God as the ultimate source of all encouragement, and he calls us to comfort others with the comfort we receive from God. Which would be a grand idea . . . if God were the One we always went to for comfort. In practice though, He often does not make our list.

Instead we tune into "this program" or pull out "that book." We call "someone who can sympathize" or visit "that person who has been there." We may talk about God's comfort but personally view it as more of a sentimental card than a saving reality. "But He is God and we are human. Can He really understand?" Oh yes, He understands—more than we possibly could know.

Can God know what it is like to be poor or have need? Yes. Jesus once summed up His personal assets by saying, *"Foxes have holes and birds of the air have nests, but the Son of Man has no place to lay his head."* (Matt. 8:20) Financial advisors would not have been impressed with Jesus' net worth. He owned little and gave away much to save a few. Jesus was entirely dependent on His Father God to provide for Him each and every day.

Does God understand what it feels like to disappoint or have conflict with your family? Yes. As a boy, Jesus' parents did not always understand Him: *"Mary said to him, 'Son, why have you treated us like this?'"* (Luke 2:48) As an adult, Scripture records that, *"even his own brothers did not believe in him."* (John 7:5) And once, his family *"went to take charge of him, for they said, 'He is out of his mind.'"* (Mark 3:21) Jesus is definitely familiar with family conflict. He felt the pain of parental disappointment and sibling disbelief.

Does God have any idea what it is like to be abused?

Yes. During His trials, Jesus was publicly stripped of His clothing, verbally mocked, and brutally beaten. He understands what it is like to suffer emotional and physical abuse and humiliation.

Does God know what it is like to have marital trouble? Yes. God often uses the imagery of marriage to describe the relationship He has with us, His often unfaithful people: *"I remember the devotion of your youth, how as a bride you loved me. . . . What fault did your fathers find in me, that they strayed so far from me? . . . You have lived as a prostitute with many lovers."* (Jer. 2:2, 5; 3:1) God knows what it is like for love to grow cold and bitter.

Does God know what it is like to grieve? Yes. *"For God so loved the world that he gave his one and only Son."* (John 3:16) Father God stood by as His Son died a painful death. He knows loss, He is well acquainted with grief. God had to bury His only Child.

Can He possibly understand what it feels like to have sinned? Yes. Not because He sinned, but because He took our sins upon His body on the cross: *"He himself bore our sins in his body on the tree, so that we might die to sins and live for righteousness."* (1 Pet. 2:24) Jesus has personally felt every sin ever committed from the little boy who did not tell the truth to the unmentionable acts of disturbed criminals. Before we even sinned, He knew our sin (and paid for it) in His body.

Need, conflict, abuse, disappointment, grief, failure . . . God fully understands all that we face in this life. The comfort He offers is real, not theoretical; actual, not sentimental. In fact, no one and no thing can comfort us more effectively than God. He will use the books and the programs and the people to help us. But He also offers us Himself. Which will we call upon first?

Other sources can help us for a moment or even a season, but God's comfort brings eternal encouragement to our souls.

☼ *God's comfort is a saving reality, not a sentimental card.*

☼ *God fully comprehends all our pain and wounds.*

☼ *Only God's comfort can penetrate and soak into the depths of our souls.*

THE COMFORTER

"I will ask the Father, and he will give you another Counselor to be with you forever—the Spirit of truth."
—JOHN 14:16–17

No study of God's comfort would be complete without a study of the Comforter Himself.

The apostle John records a series of messages Jesus gave immediately before His betrayal, trials, and crucifixion. Jesus had repeatedly tried to prepare His rather confused disciples for the difficult times ahead. In John 16, Jesus explains that though He would soon leave them, they would never be left alone:

> *"Because I have said these things, you are filled with grief. But I tell you the truth: It is for your good that I am going away. Unless I go away, the Counselor will not come to you; but if I go, I will send him to you."* (John 16:6–7)

Paraklētos is translated by various versions as

Counselor, Advocate, Helper, and Comforter. As a common noun, *paraklēsis* appears in the New Testament most often as *encouragement* or *comfort*. Jesus refers to the Holy Spirit as the divine embodiment of counsel, help, and comfort.

How does the Spirit of God comfort, counsel, and help us? For that question, let us consider Jesus' teachings on the person and work of the Holy Spirit.

"I will ask the Father, and he will give you another Counselor to be with you forever." (John 14:16) God's Spirit comforts us by *being with us.* Jesus promised the disciples that they would not be orphaned; the Spirit of truth would be with them. We cannot touch or walk with Jesus as did the early disciples. But the same Spirit of God they knew touches and walks with us.

"The Counselor, the Holy Spirit . . . will teach you all things and will remind you of everything I have said to you." (John 14:26) God's Spirit counsels us by being our teacher and reminding us of Jesus' words. God sent us a spiritual tutor with a perfect memory! That is good news—especially for those of us whose memory has recently become a little less than perfect. The Holy Spirit knows every word Jesus ever spoke and He knows every thought we ever think. So He is able to match our most

personal needs with Jesus' most pertinent truth. What a wonderful teacher He is!

"When the Counselor comes . . . he will testify about me." (John 15:26) God's Spirit helps us by testifying about Jesus. In the Greek, *testify* is translated from *martyreō,* which means *to bear witness* or *give testimony.* Jesus' teaching regarding the Holy Spirit's work follows some not-so-encouraging news. Jesus has just informed His disciples that the world will hate and persecute them (John 15:18–25). But, they will not be alone. They are to witness in this hostile world and the Holy Spirit will be testifying about Jesus right alongside them. It takes more than human words to soften a calloused soul! Jesus tells His followers that in the Holy Spirit, they have a witnessing partner: *"When he comes, he will convict the world of guilt in regard to sin and righteousness and judgment."* (John 16:8)

"He will guide you into all truth. He will not speak on his own; he will speak only what he hears, and he will tell you what is yet to come." (John 16:13) The Holy Spirit comforts us by faithfully leading us into truth. He can see clearly in the thickest fog of deception. He can steer safely through the rockiest emotional valley. He is our Guide, and He never strays from the path of truth. The Holy Spirit speaks what He hears God speaking and,

since He listens in on God's plans, He can *"tell us what is to come."* In Him, we have an absolutely reliable navigator who knows the future and never becomes disoriented!

"He will bring glory to me by taking from what is mine and making it known to you." (John 16:14) The Holy Spirit counsels us by continuing to teach us about Jesus. The disciples had only been with Jesus a few short years and their minds were filled with unanswered questions and even misconceptions. But Jesus tells them that even after His departure they will continue to grow in their knowledge of Him tutored by the Holy Spirit. God's Spirit was not sent to draw our attention away from Jesus but to increase our intimacy with Jesus.

The Comforter has come! His agenda is clear: The Holy Spirit will bring glory to Jesus in us and through us in a waiting world.

☼ *Jesus did not leave us as orphans; He sent us the Holy Spirit!*

☼ *God's Spirit is a wise tutor who guides us into all truth.*

☼ *As we walk in step with God's Holy Spirit, glory is brought to Jesus.*

WHERE IS GOD WHEN WE GRIEVE?

Jesus wept.
—JOHN 11:35

An odd company seems to surround us when we are grieving.

First, there are *the concerned but clumsy* whose desire to help is sabotaged by some inner compulsion to say something. They offer awkward, hollow, often trite advice . . . as if a single phrase could make the pain go away. Though sincere, their simplistic comments only amplify our sense of isolation in the midst of unexplainable pain.

Second, there are *the emotionally absent* who believe that loss is best forgotten. More comfortable with denial than reality, they hope that if they act as if nothing happened, we will too. The emotionally absent view more than momentary displays of grief as weakness or even a lack of faith.

Third, there are *the truly healing* who, thankfully, know that no words can banish or dilute our pain. They offer their silent, faithful, near presence. The truly healing people are simply and profoundly with us.

And then there is *God*. What posture does He assume when we are grieving?

Consider Jesus' interaction with a mourning family in John 11. Lazarus and his two sisters, Mary and Martha, lived in Bethany and were dearly loved friends of Jesus. When Lazarus became sick, the sisters sent word to Jesus. But by the time He arrived, Lazarus had already been in the tomb four days.

In studying John 11, our attention is often drawn either to the beginning of the story (Jesus' delay in coming to the sisters) or to the end of the story (Lazarus' resurrection from the dead.) But for the moment, let us pause in between and examine Jesus' role not as "God, whom we call upon" or "God, who works miracles" but simply as "God, friend of hurting hearts."

How does Jesus respond to the sisters' grief? As soon as Martha hears that Jesus has arrived, she goes to meet him on the edge of town and says, *"Lord if You had been here, my brother would not have died"* (John 11:21). It is important to emphasize what Jesus does not say in response to her. He does not say, "You shouldn't feel that way," or "How dare you accuse or question me," or "It's in the past, move on," or "Be careful or something worse may happen." Jesus responds with something true, not trite, something gracious, not judgmental: *"Your brother will rise again. . . . I am the resurrection and the life. He who believes in me will live, even though he dies."* (John 11:23, 25)

Martha returns home and secretly tells her sister that Jesus has come. Leaving quickly, Mary goes to Jesus, falls at his feet, and echoes the words of her sister: *"Lord, if you had been here, my brother would not have died."* (John 11:32)

When a grieving friend weeps at Jesus' feet, He is neither emotionally absent nor concerned but clumsy: *"When Jesus saw her weeping, and the Jews who came with her weeping, He groaned in the spirit and was troubled. And He said, 'Where have you laid him?' They said to Him, 'Lord, come and see.' Jesus wept."* (John 11:33–35, NKJV)

Where is God when we are grieving? The same place he was for Mary and Martha: with us, by the silent tomb, weeping.

Then why doesn't He say something? Why doesn't He attempt to explain our loss or lesson the pain? Perhaps because God is a *truly healing* friend who knows that no words can banish our grief.

As our hearts break, God comes close, He is not

absent. Respecting our pain, He is emotionally compassionate, not verbally clumsy.

While we grieve, God offers His silent, faithful, near presence. Like a wise, good, *truly healing* friend, He is simply and profoundly with us.

And though we cannot see or feel them, His tears mingle with ours as we weep.

☼ *God's silence is like that of a truly healing friend.*

☼ *When we grieve, He is simply and profoundly with us.*

☼ *His Presence, felt or unfelt, comforts our souls with His tears.*

RESTING IN
GOD'S GUIDANCE

~

OUR PLANS, GOD'S STEPS

A man's heart plans his way, but the LORD directs his steps.
—PROVERBS 16:9, NKJV

Finally, it was time to go! Paul's heart raced as he thought of the intended route: first through Syria and Cilicia to strengthen the churches and relay the decisions and directions of Jerusalem's leaders. Then on to Asia and Bithynia to share the truth of Jesus in new lands! Paul took a deep breath, "Thank you Jesus," he whispered, "it has always been my dream to preach the gospel where You are not yet known."

His cloak folded, his parchments prepared, Paul sat down to wait for Silas. "New sandals, but the same faithful cloak," he mused as his thoughts drifted back to his first missionary journey. That confrontation with Elymas the sorcerer in Paphos . . . the overwhelming response of both Jews and Gentiles in Psidian Antioch . . . God's miracles in Iconium and Lystra . . . and—Paul remembered with pain—John Mark's desertion in Perga . . . being stoned in Lystra . . . and now, this conflict with Barnabas.

Paul winced, "This was not my plan Lord Jesus, but I believe that You will order my steps."

Silas rapped a little too loudly at the door, his face beaming with excitement. Though a seasoned leader and prophet, Silas was both honored and thrilled to be chosen by Paul as his traveling companion. Opening the door Paul smiled and thought to himself, *"Last time I was the younger, this time the elder. My Lord, grant me the patience of Barnabas!"* After committing their path to God, the two began walking north toward Syria.

Passing into Cilicia, they stopped in Derbe and then Lystra where Timothy joined them. Together they set out with joy for Asia but were *"forbidden by the Holy Spirit to preach the word"* there (Acts 16:6, NKJV). So they tried to enter Bithynia, *"but the Spirit of Jesus did not permit them"* (Acts 16:7, NKJV).

Centuries later, we read the rest of the story and know that God redirected Paul and his companions to Macedonia where one of the most amazing stories recorded in Acts would occur. But for a few moments, let us pause with Paul, Silas, and Timothy outside the closed door of their original dreams.

From the text, we do not know exactly how the Spirit stopped the trio from entering Asia and Bithynia. It could have been another spectacular vision or a small inner witness, uncontrollable circumstances or uncooperative border patrols. But by some means, the Holy Spirit made it clear that their way was not His way, this time.

As the three turned from Paul's intended path and headed west to Troas, perhaps Silas was the first to speak: "I don't understand this. We mapped out this route in prayer." Or maybe Timothy wondered aloud, "Why wouldn't God want us to preach the gospel here? Is anyone else confused?"

Sometimes God corners us. Through disappointment, closed doors, conflict, or unwanted events, He cuts off routes we were planning on taking so He can reposition us. As we yield to His repositioning, God draws our attention to opportunities we might never have considered.

Along with Silas and Timothy, Paul no doubt felt disappointment. But the fact that his plans were not God's plans did not paralyze him spiritually. He neither returned home nor repented. His actions reveal his attitude: *he kept going* as if to say, "This is definitely not what I had planned, but I will not waste time sitting and sulking in front of a closed door." Paul knew what the writer of Proverbs 16:9 knew: We make our plans and God guides our steps. This truth gave Paul the confidence to dream, to plan, to adjust, and to keep going.

Like Paul we too can dream, strategize, and act knowing that God will close doors no one can open, open doors no one can close, and guide us faithfully into His will.

☼ *Sometimes God reroutes us into His path through disappointment.*

☼ *Divinely closed doors are not symbols of failure but of God's direction towards different opportunities.*

☼ *We can plan in confidence knowing that God will faithfully guide our steps.*

GUIDANCE FROM ABOVE

Many, O LORD my God, are the wonders you have done.
The things you planned for us no one can recount to you;
were I to speak and tell of them, they would be too many
to declare.

—PSALM 40:5

Beautiful people, fascinating culture, and a crazy city! Winding, muddy roads, missing or mangled street signs, chickens on buses, and pigs on the porch . . . On the ground it felt like chaos. But not from above. Rising over the land on the plane trip back home, suddenly planning was revealed. There was an order after all. Chaos turned to choreography from a different—and higher—perspective.

The same is true in our lives. Down here, on the ground, life often seems like a mess. But from above, God is working out His plans for us. Looking around in confusion, we shake our heads and faithfully recite God's promise: *"I know the plans I have for you, plans to prosper you and not to harm you, plans to give you hope and a future."* (Jer.

29:11) "Okay God," we think, "I am looking forward to seeing how all *this* is a part of Your plan!"

No doubt Mary and Joseph felt the same way . . . on the ground.

Thankfully, the angel Gabriel visited them both to announce and explain the coming birth of their miraculously conceived son, or else they might have experienced more than a little interpersonal tension during Mary's pregnancy. But even with the assurance they received, certainly they must have wondered about God's timing as they journeyed seventy miles from Nazareth to Bethlehem: "Did the angel tell you WHY God was going to allow Caesar to issue a census and require everyone to return to their hometown NOW when the baby is due?!" Does anybody have a plan? Actually, yes . . . but it is hard to see on the ground.

Another disappointment awaited Joseph and Mary when they attempted to find a private, clean place for the birth of their baby. Bethlehem was overflowing with out-of-town visitors and there was, *"no room for them in the inn."* (Luke 2:7) So Joseph tried to make Mary as comfortable as possible in a cave-stable or animal pen under some home. The angelic advance team surely messed up this one. They should have had a suite booked a year in advance. Not even a fruit basket awaited the holy couple.

SITTING IN GOD'S SUNSHINE

So the Savior of the world was born amidst the noises and smells of animals. Mary *"wrapped him in cloths and placed him in a manger."* Jesus' first crib was a feeding trough. Does anyone have a plan?! Actually, yes . . . but it is hard to see from the ground.

Then their first visitors arrived. Not friends, or family, but strangers. An angel appeared to a few shepherds and said, *"Today in the town of David a Savior has been born to you; he is Christ the Lord."* (Luke 2:11) The shepherds hurried into Bethlehem to see Jesus. When they left they told everyone, "The Savior has been born! He is the son of some out-of-town guests from Nazareth. You can find him in the feeding trough at the underground stables!" Does anyone have a plan?! Actually, yes . . . but it is hard to see from the ground.

From a mother's perspective, traveling during the last few months of pregnancy was not preferable. Why not stay home in Nazareth? From a father's perspective, watching your wife go through labor on a bed of mucky hay was miserable. Bethlehem was simply too crowded to host the Savior's birth. And from the watching world's perspective, a different city might have offered more prominent visitors than the shepherds, which would have added a bit more weight to that first press release. Does anybody have a plan?! Actually, yes. One foretold 700 years earlier by the prophet Micah,

> *But you, Bethlehem Ephrathah, though you are small among the clans of Judah, out of you will come for me one who will be ruler over Israel, whose origins are from of old, from ancient times.* (Micah 5:2)

But that is hard to see on the ground. Jesus' birth in Bethlehem fulfilled Messianic prophecy. Chaos on the ground was actually divine choreography from above.

We, too, often wonder "why" at God's timing, "where" at God's placement, "whom" at God's visitors. But one day, the mess on the ground will make sense. From above, we will see His masterpiece and marvel at how our lives were really a part of something much bigger and more magnificent than we could possibly have imagined.

Does anybody have a plan? Actually, yes. One day we will see it . . . from above.

☼ *God is always working out His plans for our lives.*

☼ *Mess turns to masterpiece in God's faithful hands.*

☼ *God's choreography is magnificent!*

BITTER OR BETTER?

For to me, to live is Christ and to die is gain.

—PHILIPPIANS 1:21

T he challenges we face continually change as we journey through this life. Whether we live many years or
our days are shortened by sickness or injury, we can be
confident that Satan will not retire before we do. At
every age we will be tempted with disobedience.

All of us have been in the presence of people who
have sweetened with time and people who have soured
with time. Certainly neither condition appeared overnight.
So what makes the difference? Why do some end better
and others end bitter?

We see in the apostle Paul a man who finished well.
His letter to the Philippian church was probably written
from a Roman prison around A.D. 60, seven or eight
years before his death. In his words we find attitudes
and actions that guided him, and can help guide us, to
end well.

Cultivate a prayerful heart: *"I thank my God every*

time I remember you. In all my prayers for all of you, I always pray with joy." (Phil. 1:3–4) Paul never underestimated the ministry of intercession. His letters are filled with sincere prayers for others. Prison life, no doubt, afforded him more time to focus on prayer. But having more time in itself is no guarantee of a prayerful life. A truly prayerful heart is only cultivated by discipline.

See the cup as half full: *"Now I want you to know, brothers, that what has happened to me has really served to advance the gospel."* (Phil. 1:12) Paul examined his chains and saw the gracious hand of God. Because of his restrictions, the palace guard heard about Jesus and previously timid disciples risked sharing God's truth. Those who remain sweet in spirit spend more time rejoicing over what *is* than complaining about what *is not*.

Release the unresolved: *"[Some] preach Christ out of selfish ambition, not sincerely, supposing that they can stir up trouble for me while I am in chains. But what does it matter?"* (Phil. 1:17–18) Some people just did not like Paul. Even when he was in prison, they still tried to cause him pain. But Paul refused to let other's sourness infect him. A wise saint once said, "People come with their stuff and they will leave with their stuff. You did not give it to them and you cannot take it away." Paul let the "stuff" go.

Value people more than things: *"My brothers, you whom I love and long for, my joy and crown. . . ."* (Phil. 4:1) Paul's letters clearly reveal a man who valued relationships above all earthly goods. Paul did not spend his final years fearfully counting, collecting, and protecting his assets. People, not possessions, were his true treasure. Paul spent the best of his energy investing his time, resources, and wisdom in others, and we still enjoy the fruit of that investment today.

Focus on the future: *"But one thing I do: Forgetting what is behind and straining toward what is ahead, I press on toward the goal to win the prize for which God has called me heavenward in Christ Jesus."* (Phil. 3:13–14) Even in the last few years of his life, Paul focused his thoughts on what was ahead. Several other options existed. He could have mourned his mistakes and regretted lost opportunities. He could also have lived in the land of daydreams, reminiscing about his past triumphs. Instead, Paul wrote a resignation letter to self-pity and self-love, left his failures and successes behind him, and allowed his heart to be captured by his heavenward calling.

Paul's life demonstrated his belief that, *"to live is Christ and to die is gain."* As we follow his example, we too will stay sweet to the very, very end.

☼ *Temptation never retires or resigns from our lives.*

☼ *Our own choices determine whether we become bitter or better with time.*

☼ *Sweet endings are the legacy of prayerful, positive, loving hearts.*

WAITING FOR ONE DAY

The LORD your God is with you.

—ZEPHANIAH 3:17

Prophets had a tough job in the Bible. They were often like doctors with mostly bad news. "There is spiritual cancer in this place!" they would cry. "So repent, turn back to God, and be healed!"

Zephaniah was no exception. He prophesied during the reign of good King Josiah and penned the book that bears his name around 630 B.C. God sent him to the decaying kingdom of Judah to say, "Dark days are coming, and you are the ones who snuffed out the lamp."

Of the fifty-three verses of this book, all but fifteen speak of the judgment that was coming upon the rebellious who *"rejoice in their pride."* (Zeph. 3:11) In the remaining verses, Zephaniah offers hope for the future to the humble, the repentant, and those who trust in God's name.

The prophet tells this remnant that *one day* God will lead them to a land by the sea where He will care for them. *One day* they will be able to lie down again without fear. *One day* God will rescue them and deal with their oppressors. *One day . . .*

But what were the repentant to do in between the coming day of judgment and that hoped for *one day*? What are *we* to do in difficult times while we wait in hope for God's promises to be fulfilled?

The first two chapters of Zephaniah primarily emphasize what God was about to do, but in the third chapter the prophet also speaks of who God is. Here, in Zephaniah 3:5 and 3:17, he identifies seven truths about God's character that the people of his day could hold on to as they waited for God's deliverance.

The LORD . . . is righteous; he does no wrong. God's decisions are right. His ways are entirely pure. Regardless of what is going on around us, we need to remember that God has always been and will always be thoroughly good.

Morning by morning he dispenses his justice, and every new day he does not fail. God is just. He misses nothing; His eyes see all. Evil cannot extinguish the light of His justice. Overcast skies may hide the sun, but they cannot stop its rising. In the same way, even when injustice seems to cloud the day, we can be confident that God's justice still shines brightly and He will have the final say.

The LORD your God is with you. We are not alone. God

does not abandon ship even in the roughest of seas. No matter what comes our way, He will stay with us. In the midst of a storm, we can be certain that the Creator of the Universe is steadily by our side.

He is mighty to save. God has the power to deliver us. He is an undefeated Warrior who never grows weary. The battle has not weakened our God. Though we may be exhausted, His strength is still more than sufficient to save us.

He will take great delight in you. Our days may not be delightful, but our God still delights in us. Difficult circumstances do not lesson the great joy He has in His children. Knowing that our lives bring God joy gives us the courage to walk through troubled times.

He will quiet you with his love. We often feel the physical effects of stressful seasons. Our hearts beat faster, our thoughts are filled with concerns. Here, Zephaniah teaches us that God is able to calm the storm within us. God's love—His acceptance of us and affection for us—is able to bring peace to our tense bodies and anxious minds.

He will rejoice over you with singing. The word translated *rejoice* derives from a root that means *to circle around.* God circles us with joy-filled songs of triumph! Long before we see victory with the eyes of our spirit, God rejoices over our lives. He sees the end from the beginning. Even when the way seems hidden to us, God knows that on the other side is victory!

The unchanging character of God is the anchor of enduring faith. For the remnant of Zephaniah's time, and for us, clinging tightly to these seven truths strengthens all who follow God to wait in hope for *one day*.

☼ *God's trustworthy character can keep us as we wait for His promised deliverance.*

☼ *God is able to quiet tired minds.*

☼ *Our unfailing God does no wrong and is always with us.*

THE HOLY MAN IN
CAMEL'S HAIR

*Among those born of women there has not risen anyone
greater than John the Baptist.*

—MATTHEW 11:11

"I am not the first prophet to call people to these waters," John reflected as he stepped into the Jordan. Nine centuries earlier, Elisha had called leprous Naaman to wash in the river and be healed. The army commander humbled himself and that day found complete cleansing. (2 Kings 5:14–15)

John thought of Elisha, Naaman, and the spiritual leprosy that afflicted his generation. He scanned the bank studying those who, like Naaman of old, had come to the waters. "They have come. But will they humble themselves and be cleansed?" John wondered.

Standing there, John felt the increasing weight of his now soaking clothes but they were light compared to the burden he felt in his heart: God was weeping for His people. "God has guided me to this moment. I will not fail to speak His words." With that silent affirmation, John raised his strong arms toward the heavens and cried out, "Repent and be baptized, for the kingdom of heaven is near!"

Jesus later stated that, *"among those born of women there has not risen anyone greater than John the Baptist."* How did God lead John into such greatness? Several principles of God's guidance are revealed in a study of this unusual man.

God's guidance begins even before our birth. For decades, Zechariah and Elizabeth prayed for a child and served God faithfully without one. Zechariah was in the temple one day when an angel appeared and told him he would soon have a son. This angel gave Zechariah specific instructions for how he and Elizabeth were to guide John in the ways of the Lord. He also spoke of John's future: he would be a great prophet going before the Lord to turn the people back to God.

Some, like John, are blessed with rich spiritual heritages. They can easily look through their family history and see God's hand guiding people and events that would affect their lives. But the same is true for those who did not grow up in families of faith. Whether or not our parents received angelic visitations announcing our birth, God has known and been working out His plans for us for generations.

God's guidance may seem like a mystery to a watching world. John was different. His diet was slightly more organic than his peers. Instead of bread and wine, John ate locusts and wild honey. And he took fashion cues from Elijah the prophet, dressing himself in camel's hair with a leather belt around his waist.

He was probably identifying with the prophecy that he would minister, *"in the spirit and power of Elijah."* (Luke 1:17) However, before John's prophetic ministry became evident to all, eating bugs and dressing in camel's hair probably seemed a little odd.

But John was not different for difference sake. Nor was he making a statement against others who did not prefer locusts or thought camel hair a bit uncomfortable. Obedience, not uniqueness, was John's life-goal. God's guidance led him, as it often leads us, to make some unusual choices that no doubt seem a mystery to the watching world.

God's guidance can lead us right into a desert. The desert was not punishment for John, it was preparation. In fact, it was home: *"The child grew and became strong in spirit; and he lived in the desert until he appeared publicly to Israel."* (Luke 1:80) Though this verse takes about six seconds to read, it took thirty years to live. After three decades in the desert, John's next permanent address was Herod's prison where he remained until his tragic death.

Today we have this fluffy notion that God's guidance should always lead us into bigger and better places with increasingly beautiful views. But John's life demonstrates that God in His goodness sometimes guides his people into deserts.

God's guidance leads us to decrease and Him to increase. John spent every moment of his brief public ministry preparing people for—and pointing people toward—Jesus. He considered himself a joy-filled friend of the only Bridegroom: *"He must become greater; I must become less."* (John 3:30)

The people followed John's humble example into the waters of repentance. Untold souls confessed their sins and were baptized by the holy man in camel's hair. Like Naaman, they arose from the waters cleansed; their lives changed by the obedience of an unusual man whom God guided into true spiritual greatness.

☼ *Long before our births, God was making plans for our lives.*

☼ *In His goodness, those plans may lead us into deserts.*

☼ *Regardless of the scenery, God's plans always guide us into more of Him.*

THIS IS GOOD?

And we know that all things work together for good to those who love God, to those who are the called according to His purpose.

—ROMANS 8:28, NKJV

Falsely accused, stripped naked, beaten with rods, flogged severely, imprisoned in a high security inner cell, and tortured in stocks—in Acts 16, we find Paul and Silas in a Philippian jail.

A few years later in A.D. 57, Paul would write: *"And we know that all things work together for good to those who love God, to those who are the called according to His purpose."*

Really?

God causes all things to work together for our good? Has Paul lost his short-term memory?!

Whether or not we actually believe this verse greatly depends on our definition of *good* and our understanding of *His purpose*. So let us return to Acts 16 to gain insight into these concepts through Paul's experience in Philippi.

While sharing the truth about Jesus, Paul and his

companions were shadowed by a troubled young slave girl who was *"possessed with a spirit of divination"* (Acts 16:16, NKJV). When Paul set the girl free in Jesus' name, her owners became furious because they had been making money from her fortune-telling. They dragged Paul and Silas into the marketplace and stirred up the crowd to falsely accuse them before the authorities.

Thrown into jail, beaten, bleeding, bruised, and bound in stocks, Paul and Silas began to pray and sing hymns at midnight. Listening to their worship, the other prisoners suddenly felt the ground buckle violently. A great earthquake shook the jail, broke off chains, and opened the prison doors (Acts 16:25–26).

As the jailer awoke to see the open gates, time stood still. Immediately he knew that he was a dead man. If a jailer lost a prisoner, his life was taken as repayment for his failure. Realizing the shame and agony his family would soon face, he drew a sword and pointed it at himself.

One second from suicide, the jailer heard a voice that was life itself: *"Do yourself no harm,"* Paul shouted, *"for we are all here."* Dropping his sword, the jailer ran into Paul's cell and fell on his face. *"Sirs,"* he trembled, *"what must I do to be saved?"* (Acts 16:28–30, NKJV)

Is this *good*? Yes, this is *good*.

Paul's definition of *good* did not contain a "no beatings or torture" clause. Exemption from suffering and humiliation were not his prerequisites to "the good life." In fact, *good* for Paul had little to do with his own well-being and a lot to do with the opportunity to partner with God's purpose.

We cannot separate part one from part two of Romans 8:28. Paul loved God. His life was centralized around God's call and purpose. What was God's purpose? Paul knew that answer firsthand: to set captives free.

Though in prison, Paul and Silas understood that they were not the real prisoners. Their bodies may have been broken but their souls had already been set free! And their singular pursuit was to know God and cooperate with God's purpose that other captives would be released from their prisons of sin and self.

We too are called by God to partner with Him as He sets prisoners free. Though all circumstances may not feel good, they can all work for the good of our calling in God's purpose!

So when God's guidance leads us into painful situations, like Paul and Silas we need to look around. Captives are near. Pain often places us in proximity with others who desperately need God. As they listen to our prayers, hear our worship, and see God's acts, they too—like the inmates and jailer in Paul and Silas's Philippian prison—will be freed from bondage by Jesus' saving grace.

And that would be very, very, *good*.

☼ *The good life for God's children is based on God's purposes not our own comfort.*

☼ *God calls us to partner with Him to see prisoners set free.*

☼ *Circumstances that do not feel good can still work together for God's saving purpose in the world.*

RESTING IN
GOD'S FAITHFULNESS

~

THE LAMP THAT STILL BURNS

You are my lamp, O LORD; the LORD turns my darkness into light.

—2 SAMUEL 22:29

Darker than space.

Darker than night.

The darkness spoken of by King David in 2 Samuel refers to the absolute absence of all light.

In the Hebrew, *darkness* is a translation of the word *hošek*, which makes its first biblical appearance in the creation account: *"Now the earth was formless and empty, darkness was over the surface of the deep, and the Spirit of God was hovering over the waters."* (Gen. 1:2)

This same word is later used to describe the supernatural darkness sent as a plague over Egypt: *"Then the LORD said to Moses, 'Stretch out your hand toward the sky so that darkness will spread over Egypt—darkness that can be felt.'"* (Exod. 10:21)

Some of us, like David, are well acquainted with *darkness* that can be felt. This kind of lightless-ness does not emerge from minor office misunderstandings or bad hair days. Felt darkness does not emanate from inconvenience but from intense, often prolonged pain: the death of loved ones, the betrayal of near ones, illness, lost dreams, emotional exhaustion, physical or financial collapse.

The timing of David's words in 2 Samuel 22:29 is significant. Had he written about darkness in the first chapters of his life we all would have nodded politely with knowing smiles. But David wrote this famous song of praise in the final chapters of his life. Over his seventy years, David had certainly earned the right to speak about darkness.

He was familiar with the darkness that grows from a family doubting him and a leader hating him. He knew the darkness of political wars and spiritual failures. He understood the darkness that flows from the death of babies and the betrayal of sons.

And he emerged from decades of familiarity with darkness confident in the faithfulness of his God: *"You are my lamp, O LORD; the LORD turns my darkness into light."*

In the darkness, David did not think that light would come from healing, reconciliation, deliverance, perfection, or even peace. Only one Light is powerful enough to cut through the darkness and that is God, Himself.

When David repeats this song in the Psalms he adds, *"You, O Lord, **keep my lamp burning;** my God turns my darkness into light."* (Ps. 18:28) God's lamp never runs out of oil. His light does not flicker for a moment, it endures for a lifetime.

Here again we find a parallel with the Genesis account. The same Hebrew word translated *keep burning* appears as *light* in Genesis 1:3 when God responded to the darkness:

> *And God said, "Let there be **light**," and there was* **light**. *God saw that the **light** was good, and he separated the **light** from the darkness.* (Gen. 1:3–4)

God has been bringing light into darkness for quite some time—and His Light never goes out.

The Lamp of God *kept burning* for David through over a decade of suffering under Saul's rage and jealousy. The Lamp of God *kept burning* for David even during the years of darkness he invited through his sin with Bathsheba. The Lamp of God *kept burning* for David, even when his own son tried to take the throne. That same enduring Lamp of God still burns brightly today.

Though the darkness feels overwhelming to us, it is familiar to God. He can see in the dark. More importantly,

He can speak in the dark. He can speak into the darkness of our depression. He can speak into the darkness of our failures. He can even speak into the darkness we inherit through other people's sin.

As it was in the beginning, as it was for King David, it will be for us: our faithful God will continue to turn darkness into light.

:Ö: *Though the darkness feels overwhelming to us, it is familiar to God.*

:Ö: *God can see and speak in the darkness.*

:Ö: *His voice turns darkness to light.*

ONE HUNDRED PERCENT PURE

*You, O LORD, are a compassionate and gracious God, slow
to anger, abounding in love and faithfulness.*

—PSALM 86:15

Shopping for groceries, we pick up a block of "butter"
and read a mysterious word: REAL. "But what does
it mean?" we wonder. And we should wonder in a day
when many things proclaim to be *real*, *pure*, and *genuine*
but few things actually are *real*, *pure*, and *genuine*.

After years of navigating through misleading advertising, we, the savvy consumer, have developed the *gift of suspicion*. It serves us well as we raise our brows, tilt our
heads, then squint our eyes to wisely read the labels, smell
the produce, and ask the questions necessary to determine
how phony this particular brand of *imitation* really is.

So perhaps it is understandable that our gift of suspicion does not automatically set itself on pause when we
pick up the Bible and read, *"You, O LORD, are a compassionate and gracious God, slow to anger, abounding in love and
faithfulness."* "But what does *compassionate and gracious*

really mean?" we wonder. "How slow is *slow*? How much is *abounding*?"

But here, finally, we encounter the genuine article. What we read is who God actually and always *is*. In fact, in God we find One who is truly real, utterly pure, and eternally faithful.

Sound too good to be true? Let us read the fine print together:

God is . . . *compassionate and gracious.* What does *compassionate and gracious* really mean? The Psalmist is not simply being nice in this portrayal of God. He is quoting God's own description of Himself recorded in Exodus 34:6. God (who does not lie) said He was compassionate and gracious.

Gracious speaks of *feeling sympathy for another*, or *granting unmerited favor*. The word translated *compassionate (rahûm)* is also used to describe the loving relationship between a mother and her baby or a father and his child: *"As a father has compassion on his children, so the Lord has compassion on those who fear him; for he knows how we are formed, he remembers that we are dust."* (Ps. 103:13–14)

God is neither stoic nor stiff. He genuinely feels deep compassion for us and continually shows us favor that is more reflective of His grace than our merit.

God is . . . *slow to anger*. How slow is *slow*? Consider the context of the original quote in Exodus 34. God had miraculously delivered His people out of slavery in Egypt, parted the Red Sea, provided manna and quail for them in the desert, given them water from a rock, and defeated the Amelekites. Then God called Moses up to Mount Sinai to give him the Ten Commandments, but while Moses was away, the people began to worship a golden calf as their new god.

This self-description by God as *slow to anger* was spoken *after* (not before) the people disregarded His mercy and compassion and indulged in pagan idolatry. Did He discipline them? Oh yes, severely. But if His *anger* had been released on them, they all would have perished.

When we reflect on their rebellion then, the wickedness that permeates our times now, and the fact that humanity is still in existence, it becomes clear that *slow* means God grants more second chances than any of us would ever give.

God is . . . *abounding in love and faithfulness*. How much is *abounding*? More than all who live could ever deplete! Repeatedly throughout the Psalms, *love* and *faithfulness* are used in tandem to describe God's character:

Your love, O LORD, reaches to the heavens,
your faithfulness to the skies. (Ps. 36:5)

Great is your love, reaching to the heavens;
your faithfulness reaches to the skies. (Ps. 57:10)

Great is your love, higher than the heavens;
your faithfulness reaches to the skies. (Ps. 108:4)

Phrases like "higher than the heavens" and "reaches to the skies" would normally activate our gift of suspicion. But these words are not poetic hyperbole when used in reference to God. His faithfulness is unfathomable. His love is inexhaustible!

God's compassion, grace, patience, love and faithfulness truly endure forever: He is REAL, absolutely genuine, and always 100 percent pure!

☼ *God's self-portraits are entirely accurate.*

☼ *The compassion He has for us is genuine, felt, and full.*

☼ *God's faithfulness is like a towering mountain whose peak is beyond our grasp.*

A CHOSEN ATTITUDE

The LORD was with Joseph and he prospered.

—GENESIS 39:2

God's faithfulness is eternal, more certain than the sunrise. The Scriptures consistently affirm that faithfulness is an unchanging, everlasting component of God's character. However, the fact that God is faithful to us does not guarantee that we will be faithful to Him. Joseph adopted an attitude that enabled him to become a man of great faithfulness. In every circumstance Joseph chose to rest in the knowledge that God's good hand was on his life.

When he was seventeen, his jealous brothers sold him to merchants who in turn sold him to an Egyptian official. In a matter of days, Joseph went from being a prosperous, favored son in his father's household to the penniless slave of an unknown master. His dad thought him dead, and his brothers did not care if he was alive. But,

The LORD was with Joseph and he prospered. . . .

> *When his master saw that the LORD was with*
> *him and that the LORD gave him success in every-*
> *thing he did, Joseph found favor in his eyes and*
> *became his attendant.* (Gen. 29:2–4)

Rarely do we look at a bitter, angry individual and exclaim, "I can see that God is with you!" Josephs' attitude obviously communicated something of God's presence to his master. So it is safe to assume that not only was God faithful to Joseph, but Joseph *believed* that God was faithful to him and acted accordingly. His jealous brother's unfaithfulness did not invalidate God's faithfulness.

As time passed, Joseph had many more opportunities to rest in God's faithfulness in the midst of undesirable circumstances. Day after day in Potiphar's house, his master's wife tried to seduce Joseph but he refused *"to do such a wicked thing and sin against God."* (Gen. 39:9) Joseph paid for his integrity with his freedom and was sent to prison after the woman accused him of trying to molest her. Nevertheless,

> *While Joseph was there in the prison, the LORD*
> *was with him; he showed him kindness and*
> *granted him favor in the eyes of the prison warden.*

So the warden put Joseph in charge. (Gen. 39:20–22)

Once again, Joseph's chosen attitude reflected God's presence to those in authority. The words of Potiphar's wife had stained his reputation, but Joseph would not allow them to stain his mind. People can place our bodies in prison, but only we can place our souls in prison. Joseph kept his soul free by choosing to rest in God's faithfulness.

Years later, we find Joseph compassionately caring for other prisoners. In God's name, he interprets the dreams of two officials and asks the first,

> *"When all goes well with you, remember me and show me kindness; mention me to Pharaoh and get me out of this prison. For I was forcibly carried off from the land of the Hebrews, and even here I have done nothing to deserve being put in a dungeon."* (Gen. 40:14–15)

But,

> *The chief cupbearer, however, did not remember Joseph; he forgot him.* (Gen. 40:23)

Joseph's request reveals a man who knew he was paying the price for other people's sin. Resting in God's faithfulness did not make him numb to that pain. It did however give him perspective.

Josephs' jealous brothers had abandoned him, but that did not make God unloving. Potiphar's adulterous wife had falsely accused him, but that did not make God unjust. The king's forgetful cupbearer had failed him, but that did not make God untrustworthy. Joseph chose to distinguish between *what people did* and *Who God was*. That attitude empowered Joseph—through the trials and testing of slavery, imprisonment, and later the palace—to remain faithful to his faithful God.

☼ *Only we can place our souls in prison.*

☼ *The unfaithfulness of others does not cancel God's faithfulness.*

☼ *To remain faithful to God we must distinguish between what people do and Who God is.*

STRENGTH TO STAND

No temptation has seized you except what is common to man. And God is faithful; he will not let you be tempted beyond what you can bear. But when you are tempted, he will also provide a way out so that you can stand up under it.

—1 CORINTHIANS 10:13

For days, a steady drizzle of freezing rain fell upon the Silver Maple. At first the ice seemed benign, coating the elegant tree with a seemingly harmless shimmer. But with each additional layer, the Maple began to look more like a Willow as its long straight limbs arched in response to the increasing weight. Suddenly, the pressure was simply too much. The burden became unbearable and, with a deafening crack, the huge tree snapped as an enormous bough crashed to the ground.

Have you ever felt like you were at the breaking point in resisting temptation? Have you ever sensed your will bending toward sin and feared that it just might break?

Physically, the tree had no choice. But, spiritually we

always do. The Word of God assures us that God will never allow temptation to layer so thickly in our lives that, like the tree, we have no choice but to fall crushed beneath the burden of its weight: *"God is faithful; he will not let you be tempted beyond what you can bear."*

The apostle Paul penned this timeless truth around A.D. 56 to a group of young believers in a temptation-filled city. Corinth was a thriving crossroads of commerce that celebrated and profited from its utter abandonment of morality. When Paul and his friends brought the good news of salvation to this lawless land, many responded to Jesus' offer of forgiveness. In turning to Jesus, these new believers turned away from sexual immorality, idolatry, adultery, perversion, theft, greed, addictions, slander, and deceitful practices. (1 Cor. 6:9–10) But Satan does not politely dismiss himself when we give our lives to Jesus. He continues to try us, to tempt us, to entice us with sin. Conjuring up temptation was not difficult in a city like Corinth.

Those who had been in bondage to sexual immorality regularly passed by the thousand prostitutes of Aphrodite's temple. Those who had worshiped pagan gods no doubt dealt daily with family conflict their new faith created. Those who had been entangled in adultery still walked by the doorways of their former lovers. Recovering alcoholics were still offered drinks by their co-workers, and former thieves certainly felt the pinch when their pockets were no longer padded by crime.

Temptation continued to rain steadily on these followers of Jesus. With each successive layer, Satan tempted them to bend their will toward sin.

Sound familiar? Like these early believers, we too must work out our salvation in a lawless land. The internet may have replaced Aphrodite's temple, and self-gratification may have become our favored pagan god, but our struggles, and Satan's strategies, remain the same.

Thankfully for the Corinthians, and for us, "new life in Jesus" is not a greeting card nicety or a hollow sales-hook. Jesus died on the cross to set us free from sin and empower us to live—not just dream about—a transformed life.

In the place of temptation, Paul counsels us to hold tightly to three truths.

No temptation has seized you except what is common to man. Our struggles are not new. All humans are tempted with sin. The enemy may be sly, but he is not creative. We cannot let Satan deceive us into believing that we are all alone in a challenge that no one else has ever faced or survived. Whatever it is, it is common. Jesus has enabled His followers to resist it before and He is able to help us resist it now.

God is faithful; He will not let you be tempted beyond what you can bear. God knows our limits. In His love, He will never allow temptation to be stronger than we can endure. It may press us, but it cannot crush us.

When you are tempted, God will also provide a way out so that you can stand up under it. Temptation cannot trap us. God will always provide a way of escape. Our responsibility is to take that way and not unnecessarily expose ourselves to another icy layer of Satan's tempting.

In this life, we all experience the weight of temptation. But we are not alone in our battle against sin. The faithful Son of God, who endured temptations more fierce than we can possibly imagine, offers us His saving strength—and by that strength we will stand!

☼ *All of us struggle to resist bending toward sin.*

☼ *God will never allow that struggle to be stronger than we can bear.*

☼ *In His faithfulness, God will always provide a way out of temptation.*

O MAGNIFY!

Your path led through the sea, your way through the
mighty waters, though your footprints were not seen.

—PSALM 77:19

nseen footprints. Looking back they are easy to identify. But in the middle of a spiritual crisis, when we
see and feel nothing of God, we begin to fear that He is
no longer near.

Thankfully for us, the writers of the Bible did not edit
out the darker, doubt-filled, desperate pages of their spiritual journeys.

Somewhere between 1020 and 975 B.C., a man named
Asaph penned a pain-filled song. Asaph, a skilled musician
and seer, was one of the temple worship-leaders during
King David's reign. The circumstances that preceded the
writing of his psalm are unknown, but the phrases Asaph
uses reveal a man who urgently needed to hear from God:
"My soul refused to be comforted." "I groaned; I mused, and my
spirit grew faint." "I was too troubled to speak."

In Psalm 77, Asaph writes about a season in his life

where his soul knew famine. These seasons are not unfamiliar to us. When our prayers are met by God's extended silence, our spirits may start to feel faint. We want to believe that God is still there, but questions begin to rise within us.

Questions arose in Asaph's heart as well and he voiced them before God:

> *Will the LORD reject forever?*
> *Will he never show his favor again?*
> *Has his unfailing love vanished forever?*
> (Ps. 77:7–8)

Asaph felt spiritually disappointed. He asked sincere questions of God, but he did not stop there as we often do. In the midst of the silence, with questions still hanging in the air, Asaph chose to remember God's past faithfulness:

> *I will remember the deeds of the LORD; yes, I will*
> *remember your miracles of long ago. I will medi-*
> *tate on all your works and consider all your*
> *mighty deeds.* (Ps. 77:10–12)

We magnify what we meditate upon. Like Asaph, we can be honest about our despair and doubts. But if we only think about our pain, it will be amplified in our lives.

Asaph models for us one who, in the midst of unanswered prayers, meditated on God's character and saw trust magnified in his soul!

> *Your ways, O God, are holy. What god is so great as our God? You are the God who performs miracles; you display your power among the peoples.* (Ps. 77:13–14)

Along with Asaph, our futures are often forged by the choices we make in troubled times. Asaph's choice affected his legacy. After this spiritual crisis, Asaph went on to write many more Psalms that are still providing encouragement to us thousands of years after his death.

Asaph ached. Asaph questioned. Then he chose to remember the goodness of God. May we follow his example when God's footprints are unseen. As we meditate on God's faithfulness, faith will be magnified in our souls!

☼ *Like us, the biblical writers were familiar with doubt and despair.*

☼ *In times of crisis, we will magnify what we meditate upon.*

☼ *If we meditate on God's faithfulness, trust will be amplified in our hearts!*

ABOUT THE AUTHOR

Photo by randybacon.com

As a young atheist, Alicia Britt Chole believed that man had invented God to fill the gaps in human knowledge. "Truth to me was dead, God never lived, life was full of pain, and death was the end of life." In 1983 God captured Alicia's attention and her soul. She is now a highly respected Christian author and international speaker. Her other books include *Pure Joy* and *Until the Whole World Knows.* She has also developed a complete Bible study curriculum.

Alicia is the wife of Barry and the mother of Jonathan and Keona. They make their home in Rogersville, Missouri.

For further information about Alicia, visit
www.onewholeworld.com